VICKI MURPHY

MotherFumbler

DELIGHTFULLY TWISTED TALES FROM THE CREATOR OF
motherblogger.ca

1 Stamp's Lane, St. John's, NL, Canada, A1E 3C9
WWW.BREAKWATERBOOKS.COM

COPYRIGHT © 2013 Vicki Murphy

LIBRARY AND ARCHIVES CANADA CATALOGUING IN PUBLICATION
Murphy, Vicki, 1978-, author
MotherFumbler / Vicki Murphy.
Delightfully twisted tales from the creator of *motherblogger.ca.*
ISBN 978-1-55081-440-8 (pbk.)
1. Motherhood--Humor. 2. Parenting--Humor. I. Title.
PN6231.M68M87 2013   306.874'30207   C2013-905898-2

 Canada Council   Conseil des Arts   Canadä   Newfoundland
for the Arts   du Canada   Labrador

We acknowledge the support of the Canada Council for the Arts, which last year
invested $154 million to bring the arts to Canadians throughout the country.
We acknowledge the Government of Canada through the Canada Book Fund
and the Government of Newfoundland and Labrador through the Department of
Tourism, Culture and Recreation for our publishing activities.

PRINTED AND BOUND IN CANADA.

 MIX
Paper from
responsible sources
FSC® C016245

FOR MOM AND DAD
FROM TURBO GINGER 1.0

CHANGING TABLE OF CONTENTS

INTRODUCTION: Hell Hath No Fury Like a Woman Torn............ 9

CHAPTER ONE: Childbirth: Getting Screwed in More Ways Than One 13

Dis Bitch Ain't No Mother............ 14

To Breed or Not to Breed: Reflections of a Broken Vagina............ 18

Burn Your Birth Plan Before It Burns You............ 23

All About (Blaming) Eve............ 25

Giving Birth: Cruel and Unusual...Privilege?............ 28

Breast Is Best. It Is Also the Worst............ 30

CHAPTER TWO: Life Is a Beauty Cuntest............ 35

Ugly Baby Alert: A Face Only a Mother Could Love............ 37

Pobody's Nerfect............ 38

Get in the Goddamn Pool............ 44

Like Mother, Like Son of a Gun............ 49

This Is Epic............ 51

CHAPTER THREE: Welcome to Smotherhood............ 57

Time Waits for No Mom............ 58

A Work(ing Mother) in Progress............ 59

Basket Case............ 62

Silly Beaver............ 64

Boob-Tube Baby............ 66

Single Parents: How in the Mother Do You Do It?............ 70

Romance: Gone the Way of the Placenta............ 74

Dear Husband, Are You Fucking Blind?............ 78

CHAPTER FOUR: Playing Mommy............ 83

Working for the Geekend............ 84

Growing Up. Boo............ 87

A Toy Story............ 89

Classic Toys for Poor Kids............ 91

Hide and Seek for Dummies............ 93

Guys and Dolls............ 96

CHAPTER FIVE: Turbo Ginger............ 103

Turbo Gingers: Born Not Made 104

Travelling with Satan's Spawn 104

A Word from the Snottery 108

A Walking Nightmare 110

Kids Are Really, Really Gross. And Disgusting, Also 113

Motherhood Is the Shit 115

Rock-the-Boat Baby 118

All We Need Is Just a Little Patience 121

Shopping Maul 123

Kids Are Assholes 128

CHAPTER SIX: The Sappy Stuff 135

Growing Things 136

Immortal Beloved Words 140

I'll See You in My Dreams 142

Father, Son, and Holy Shit 145

First Born: The Furkid Gets the Shaft 148

Rain, Drizzle, Fog, and Family 151

Escape from the Hood 155

CHAPTER SEVEN: Just Another Manic Mommy 159

When the Bow Breaks 160

Crappy Easter from the Party Pooper 162

Friendship Is Hard 165

Human Skittles 168

Take Your Sperm and Shove It! 170

Shit That Blows My Mind 173

The Lord Made Me but the Devil Raised Me 175

Dear Pope: Time for a Few Tweaks 178

A Letter to Max 181

CHAPTER EIGHT: Oh Shit We're All Going to Die 185

No Bunny's Daughter 186

Cock-a-Doodle-Dead 189

Life Is a (Little Boy on a) Beach 191

Letting Go and Holding On 193

Hold On to Your Dreams. And Your Dump Truck. 198

Firemom 199

Survival: A Little Crazy Goes a Long Way 202

Mothers are all slightly insane.

— J.D. SALINGER, *THE CATCHER IN THE RYE*

Hell Hath No Fury Like a Woman Torn

The day is all a blur now, thank god.

My husband unlocked the door of the house. The dog scurried in, excited to be home after two hours of waiting in the car in the hospital parking lot. She almost knocked the baby carrier out of my hand as she beelined to her food dish to see if the pork chop gods had visited while she was out.

Andrew put my bag on the table, my blood-spattered slippers sticking out of the side pocket, and collapsed onto the couch, exhausted, like he had just given birth or something.

The house felt different somehow. Emptier. Even though it had never been so full.

I set the baby carrier on the zigzag rug and gingerly sat down in the new glider. Holy shit, there's a baby on my zigzag rug! But… why don't I hear cherub music softly playing in the background? Why isn't sunlight cascading in from the perfect world? And where the FUCK are the rainbows and butterflies?

The baby shampoo commercials. The books. It was all a lie.

Let's see….

My vagina is permanently screwed.

Thanks to my hemorrhoids, my bowel movements register on the Sphincter Scale.

Breastfeeding hurts like a son of a bitch.

I'm still wearing maternity pants. Because my ass and abs didn't get the memo.

Max's cry is the official anthem of Hades.

All my friends are at work wearing pencil skirts and making their dreams come true.

I'm broke.

My dog is sad.

My husband has more compassion for her than me. Maybe he can fuck her from now on. There's your doggy style for ya, honey.

And oh yeah, my dad is dying of cancer. Bonus.

How could I have fallen for the fairy tale? I work in advertising for frig sake; I tell fairy tales for a living.[1] But I guess I wanted this tale to be real. To have just one perfect thing in the motherfuckery.

Now that I know the truth, what do I do? I don't know…write a book?

Here's your warning. If you're looking for one of those *Chicken Soup for the Soul* books, you're staring into the wrong pot. I can't give you soup, but I can pour on the sauce. Hey, I'm a mother; nobody said I was a lady. And who wants to read a book by a lady anyways? Well, my own mother. But besides her—who?

The magical land of motherhood you see on television and read about in books and hear about from crazy-ass moms with buttons where their eyes should be—it doesn't exist. Motherhood is 50% amazeballs (I'm not a monster), but 60% nightmare. And yes, that math is correct. It takes more of you than you actually have.

And holy mother, does it ever change you. Not just your lifestyle,

---

[1] Actually, advertising is about revealing the truth. But sometimes ads focus on one truth (like babies are wonderful) and ignore all the other truths (like babies are chubby jerks) which can be misleading. The truth is, only some truths sell shit. So those are the ones we see.

but who you are, how you see the world. It's a total pantsformation. A metamorphosis that starts in your trousers. Think about it. Until childbirth, our vaginas are just there. Neatly tucked away, causing no trouble, subordinate to the supreme, ever-thinking female brain. But once a woman has given birth—BOOM! The sleeping snatch is awakened, pissed off, enraged. Hell hath no fury like a woman torn.

It's like how men think with their dicks. From the moment they wake up, there's the ol' pants soldier, standing at attention, guiding them through the day like a dangling carrot leading a donkey. Which is also called an ass. But unlike dicks, our vaginas are in pursuit of truth and justice. Dicks are in pursuit, but they just have one destination: someone else's undies.

So I guess you could say my vagina wrote this book, because the violence it suffered permeates everything I do and say and write. Like a soldier with PTSD, my GI' Gina cannot shake the gory ghosts of war. It has seen too much. It can never go back. It is my red vadge of courage in a mad, mad world.

Don't tell your kids you had an easy
birth or they won't respect you. For years
I used to wake up my daughter and say,
"Melissa, you ripped me to shreds.
Now go back to sleep."

— JOAN RIVERS

CHAPTER ONE

Childbirth: Getting Screwed in More Ways Than One

Having a baby is a double-edged sword. And feels like passing one, too. It blows your mind—and all your girly bits—to smithereens. My son is out of diapers now and every time I look at his sweet face I see the business end of a medieval spiked mace headed straight for my crotch.

All you moms out there who had a "textbook birth," who so sincerely apologize for our lesser fortune in the birthing suite, who answer "no biggie" when asked "how was it?" News flash: we hate your face.

I know you're mostly just a big ol' fur burger, but use your head too. Is "no biggie" a wise choice of words to a woman whose baby just tore her a new one? That giant crochet hook must have broke more than your water, sister, because your common sense drained out with the amniotic fluid.

This principle applies beyond childbirth. To hair, for example. Do I go around bragging about my glorious crimson mane? No, because I don't want you to feel bad about your Mount Pearl Curl[1] or

---

[1] In the 1980s, every young female in Mount Pearl, then a suburb of St. John's, had bangs hair-sprayed to the heavens to create the infamous Mount Pearl Curl. Some social outcasts still sport it today.

being an aviation blonde.[2] And most importantly, I don't want you to hate me. It's our job to hate the *men* who did this to us, remember?

Maybe you did have a decent birthing experience. You probably got the epidural and took a nap while they vacuumed the slimy meatball out of your comatose twat. Maybe you had a C-section and now have a PPP.[3] Congratufuckenlations. But guess what—at some point you must have had some discomfort, some pressure, some something. You just thrust a human into the world for Christ's sake. It doesn't come without a couple strings attached, or at least a Foley catheter.[4] So please, for the sanity of the woman whose bundle of joy sat on her sciatic nerve for four months and smashed her tailbone on the descent, and the new mama who gave birth to her bladder along with the baby—FAKE IT. Pretend it was at least a little challenging. Unless you enjoy the sensation of a doughnut pillow lodged in your windpipe. But then I guess you wouldn't feel that either, tough girl.

If you must, go knit your little hats and socks and update your Facebook status to "I am sooooo lucky, motherhood is amazing, my baby is a precious gift from God." And I will carry on nursing my panty hamster back to health, and wondering how many coats of sugar it would take for me to feel like you.

At ease, soldier.

Dis Bitch Ain't No Mother

Despite the frequent reminders from my land down under, I sometimes forget I'm a mom. I admit it. When I'm away from Max for an extended period of time—if I'm out of town shooting a TV

[2] A girl who has dyed her hair blonde. Airplanes have flight data recorders, commonly referred to as "black boxes." "Box" is slang for vagina. Hence, an "aviation blonde" is a girl with blonde hair, but with a "black box." Where do they come up with this stuff?

[3] Perfectly Preserved Pussy

[4] A Foley catheter is used to "ripen" the cervix, to induce labour. A balloon is inserted behind the cervical wall and inflated, applying pressure to the cervix, as the baby's head would, causing it to dilate. To the doctor who inserted my Foley catheter: you owe me a pair of slippers.

spot, or just shooting liqueurs off my TV set—he occasionally slips my mind. It's not that he's not close to my heart. He's my everything. But there was a time when he wasn't, because he was nothing at all. And every now and then I revert back to the old me. The me I was for thirty years. The me that was not a mother.

I never pictured myself as a mom. Maybe because I never fancied myself as much of a woman. Growing up, I was part tomboy, part ugly girl. I played with Barbie *and* GI Joe. I wore frilly blouses *and* MC Hammer pants. I was a little bit of everything all wrapped up in one. I was a Boy George burrito.

My vagina was one of the few body parts I actually liked. I explored its topography during low-budget Canadian movies on late night CBC. The rest of the anatomical package I didn't quite know what to do with. At age twelve, I had the figure of an eight-year-old boy. Not just any eight-year-old boy—the banjo boy from *Deliverance*. So when I began to sprout breasts, it just felt entirely foolish. What was the point? I was never going to use them. Boys would never touch them. Certainly no baby was ever going to suckle them. Romance and marriage and motherhood were things that would happen to other girls, not to me.

But wait a damn second. I loved to play house! That must mean something, right? And no, I did not play the role of the husband or the child. I played a pool boy named Milton Berle. Kidding. I played the wife, damn it! My friend Patty played the husband because she was tall and had short dark hair and looked like Bobby Ewing from *Dallas*. I made the mud pies and dandelion salad; she carried a broken calculator around in Dad's old briefcase. And no, we didn't make out, despite what my husband would like to imagine.

Then came a sure sign of my innate maternal instincts: the kittens. We snatched them from a couple slutty neighbourhood strays that had made themselves at home under a rundown shed. Kidnapping: a sure sign of a fit parent. We kept our fur babies locked in my playhouse in the backyard. We brought them balls of yarn. I bought cat food at the corner store with my five-dollar weekly allowance. I named them all: Fluffy, Snowball, Cuddles, and Dave. I took good care of my little brood. You know, unless I was travelling to the city with my family to get my braces adjusted, leaving the kittens in the playhouse for days on end. When we got home, I'd rush to the little wooden door and open it up to release the staggering whiff of cat food, piss, and shit.

I loved those kitties. I really did. But one day, they all disappeared. Maybe they ran away and joined the pussy circus. Maybe my grandfather pulled the ol' "pillowcase full of rocks" routine. (Shudder.) Or maybe they just went off in search of more consistent nourishment, where food, water, and belly rubs didn't depend on my hopscotch and Pogo Bal schedule.

"Where are they?" asked Patty, holding a ball of yellow wool from an old sweater my nan had unravelled that morning.

"Where are what?"

"The kittens. Fluffy and Cuddles and Snowball and Dave."

"They grew into cats and ran away."

"Geez. That was fast."

We played cat's cradle with the yarn and never spoke of the kittens again. A week later we were smoking cigarettes behind the gas station and replacing the Smurf and Muppet posters in our bedrooms with ones of Whitesnake, Harem Scarem, and Poison.

Other than some occasional babysitting in high school, the kittens were my only training for motherhood. I had no younger siblings to care for and my only pet was a rock with a face. So when I became pregnant a couple decades later at the ripe old age of thirty, part of me thought—could I actually do this? Was I even *allowed* to do this? Was there some kind of test I should take? Like, maybe a fitness test, except instead of asking me to do chin-ups and push-ups they ask things like, "Does your house have wheels?" or "Do you include estimated scratch ticket winnings in your household budget?" or "Have you ever neglected a precious baby animal, you *monster*!?" Seriously. How was I going to take care of Max if I couldn't even take care of Dave?

Slap! Pull yourself together, woman. Surely my self-doubt would subside after Max arrived. It would all come naturally to me then. Right? Like some glorious swirl of maternal wisdom whooshing up inside me, taking the place of the placenta, making everything suddenly click. *Right?*

The price is wrong, bitch. There was no whoosh. I had to slowly get the hang of changing him, feeding him, swaddling him, bathing him, and not poking my fingers through the top of his squishy head. And it sure didn't take the edge off knowing there was a cop—hello, Child Protective Services—just fifteen feet down the hall in the maternity ward! I shit you not. For my entire six-day stay at the hospital, a police officer stood guard outside the nursery, 24/7. Apparently a new mother down the hall had received death threats: the new girlfriend of her baby daddy said she was going to come to the hospital and choke the baby out. Yeah, sure you will, Glen Close in *Fatal Attraction*. But clearly they take this shit seriously. Directly across from the room full of new babies, Eliot Ness sat upright in a chair. Sometimes with a magazine, sometimes just staring at the door with his thick arms folded across his bulletproof vest. I wondered if the targeted tot was wearing a bulletproof diaper.

So he wasn't watching me, per se. But still. He was there, judging me, betting on when he'd be coming to my house to pull my kid out of the artesian well. Every three hours, I'd scuff down to the nursery to fetch my boy and wheel him back to my room to be fed from my ginormous new chesticles. Kojak just glared at me. Not a look or glance. A glare. No smile, no congratulations, no "Hey, wanna touch my gun?" Just a glare. Sheesh.

Those six days on the maternity ward would have been hard enough, let alone with a cop breathing down my robe and a psycho threatening to go postal on the postnatal. I was all drugged up. My hormones were up and down more than Charlie Sheen's zipper (#winning). Truth be told, I probably should have been staying on the psych ward. But come on, of course I was crazy! My vadge looked like the guy's face from *Mask*. I couldn't take a decent shit because my asshole was no longer functional. Or recognizable. I wasn't even sure I still had one. Ah, not like I actually needed an anus anyways since I wasn't eating enough food to speak of. They served me greasy little sausages every other day, reminding me of the wiener that got me into this mess in the first place. But hey, at least I could soak my troubles in a bubble bath. Um, no. There was no tub. What do you think this is—the Ritz? There was just a toilet, a shower, and a plastic pan in which to soak my mystery muff. And don't forget the cute little squirt bottle for cleaning my Franken'gina. You know, so I didn't wipe myself with toilet paper and tear out the stitches in my new snatchwork quilt. It was all very wonderful. And just for shits and giggles, they put Dennis Franz outside my room to watch all my comings and goings. What. The. Hell. Did I just have a baby or hijack a plane?

Just short of a week after his birth, Max's jaundice receded and we were able to go home. By then, I had the basics down pat. I was pretty sure I could keep this little person alive. Nobody stopped us when we tried to leave. Nobody tailed us home. Tyne Daley[5] was not waiting in the driveway. It looked like I was going to get another chance at this motherhood thing. And this time the little critter didn't have claws or whiskers. This time I had a baby.

Note to self: don't eff it up. And for the love of god, don't keep it in the playhouse.

To Breed or Not to Breed: Reflections of a Broken Vagina

I'm looking at Max lying in the bathtub, sliding around on his belly, his cute little arse cheeks nipped together like an angry muffin.

"Drink water," he says as he takes a gulp and grins, his upper lip sporting a thick bubble-stash.

"Drink water, drink water…"

He repeats it again and again until I warn, "Now Max, you know you're not supposed to drink the bath water. It's dirty."

He looks at me for a long time, his orange eyebrows entwining to form a question mark. One day soon he will ask, "But Mom, if the water is dirty, why am I in it?"

Touché, little dude, touché.

He is growing so fast. He's the full length of the bathtub now.

---

[5] Tyne Daly played a child protective services worker on the CBS show *Judging Amy*.

He has a moustache for god's sake! Holy shit—it must be time to have another baby.

I feel a sudden ache in my uterus and a burning in my loins. Desire? Hells no. Try the lifelong repercussions of squeezing a person out of my secret eyelid. Oh the horror.

So...do I spit out another youngster or not? I am torn. And oh how I wish that was not a play on words.

This calls for one of the things my husband dreads more than penis-kabobs and conversation—a *list*. Don't worry, honey. It's not a honey-do list. Unless it concludes with "do me," in which case I'm confident you'll stand at attention and follow orders. It's a list of pros and cons. To breed or not to breed: that is the question.

PRO: Max gets a brother or a sister.

CON: I have to *grow* said brother or sister inside my body and get it here via the Va-Jay-Jay Express.

PRO: The Bearded Oyster is already a dive, so why not close shop altogether and go home with a nice souvenir?

CON: I am well-healed and happy to be back to my pre-prego weight, despite the extra stomach skin that makes me look like an accordion when I sit down and pretty much annihilates my lifelong dream of donning a mesh crop top like Madonna in her "Lucky Star" video. Why mang all that merchandise up again?

PRO: I get an extra human to produce grandchildren for me.

CON: I have to worry that said human will produce grand-children at age thirteen.

PRO: We get a baby to love and cuddle.

CON: We get the world's tiniest fashion critic who thinks my designer threads look better with accents of piss, puke, and poop.

PRO: If it's a boy, I get to reuse all Max's perfectly unsoiled clothes.

CON: If it's a girl, I have to buy a bunch of pink clothes so our daughter doesn't look like K.D. Lang.[6]

PRO: We get to make another living, breathing masterpiece.

---

[6] I'm totally kidding. I have a constant craving for K.D.—the singer, and the macaroni and cheese. And I hate the pink and blue bullshit. How much do I hate it? See page 96.

Max is way too cute to have just one of him.

CON: Maybe Max used up all the good DNA and the next one is doomed to get the leftovers: big nose, big ears, third nipple, and eye of Cyclops.

CON: Every time I do a jumping jack at the gym, I pee a little. After kid number two, I'll have to wear a pillow-top mattress inside my underwear.

PRO: Once I'm pregnant, I can eat what I want because I'm going to get fat anyways. My pet saying as a prego? "Quarter pounder with cheese combo, upsize the fries, six nuggets on the side, and an apple pie, si vous NOW."

CON: My ass will resemble the broad side of a barn for at least six to nine months, with the possibility of permanent barnliness. On my first pregnancy, I was often mistaken for one of the livestock. The farmer down the road kept trying to herd me into his shed.

CON: Bye-bye, MILF t-shirt. Hello, saddle. My career as a swimsuit model is so over.

PRO: Cha-ching! Another kid—another thousand bucks from the Newfoundland and Labrador Government.[7]

CON: Cha-shit! The average cost of raising a child in Canada? Fourteen zillion dollars. And that's just the Goldfish crackers.

PRO: My in-laws get grandbaby number ten for a nice even number. My mom gets grandkid number four. Maybe a girl this time?

CON: Not gonna happen, sister. The walls of my uterus are painted blue. Last Tuesday, I pooped a dump truck sticker and a handful of gravel.

PRO: I get a year of maternity leave.

CON: I get a year trapped in a time warp, relying on Employment Insurance that doesn't cover shit, not even shit catchers. $42 for a box of 100 diapers? A second kid's gonna have to use the litterbox.

PRO: My husband could take paternity leave, so I could go on working.

---

[7] The Newfoundland and Labrador government rewards us for giving birth and combating the province's dwindling population. The Albertan hookers impregnated by our men working there do not qualify for this assistance.

CON: I will attempt to strangle him with the cord of Max's Fisher Price telephone every time I leave for work in the morning.

CON: Breastfeeding will deflate my boobs (even more) and I'll have to wear a super-duper-push-up bra just to keep the suckers out of my (empty) pockets.

CON: Those bras are expensive. I may just have to glue my tits to my chin.

PRO: I get to go to mommy-and-baby movies at the theatre on Thursday mornings.

CON: No I don't, because I have another kid at home crushing my dreams of being a socialite with a life, a stylist, and a sex tape.

PRO: I can get one of those kickass double strollers.

CON: I need one of those bloody double strollers. Can I borrow twenty bucks? How much can I get for this MILF t-shirt?

PRO: Max can use the baby as a pillow in the single-seater stroller. Score.

CON: Andrew and I will be so busy being parents, we'll forget about our relationship.

PRO: We'll be so busy being parents, we'll forget about our relationship problems.

PRO: When we get divorced, we get one kid apiece. No need to pull a Solomon.[8]

CON: I set my career back a notch or two. Come on people, you know it's true. One of the reasons there'll never be a young female president: we're breeders.[9]

CON: I'll never find the time to write the sequel to this book.

CON: My husband is not the doting type. So when I start getting fat and uncomfortable, I can look forward to *not* getting my feet massaged.

CON: Max is already a hell of a lot of work. As I type this, he is swinging from the bathroom doorknob with a butter knife in his

---

[8] Two women came to King Solomon of Israel with a child, both claiming to be its mother. Solomon ruled to cut the child in two to give each woman half. This clever judgment revealed the child's true mother who begged the king to spare the child's life and give him to the other woman. Solomon was one smart son-of-a-Bathsheba.

[9] There will be a female president, but she'll be post-menopausal. She'll be the head of state and hot flashes.

hand, flies in his teeth, oatmeal in his hair, and a load in his shorts.

CON: My dad was sick when I was pregnant. He died when Max was nine months old. So for me, pregnancy means impending doom. Textbook psychiatry. (I can diagnose myself because I have Internet access.)

CON: First trimester nausea. Once, on my way to work, I threw up in my hat.

CON: Second trimester semi-chubbiness when people aren't sure if you are having a baby or if you just had a big lunch. Awkward.

CON: Third trimester bulbousness when people mistake you for the Penguin from *Batman*. Followed by the awesome sensation of carrying a bowling ball in your underwear.

CON: Sleep deprivation. Max didn't sleep through the night for ten months. Lack of sleep has been known to cause psychosis in adults, as well as extreme sarcasm, profanity, and hyperbole.

CON: Vagination Ruination: the Sequel.

CON: The Meat Curtain Massacre, Part Deux.

CON: Hotdogs in Hallways: The Final Poke.

CON: Wow, that's a lot of cons. To top it off, maybe one of my kids will be a con. Max is already terrible at sharing, and goes ape-shit for toys at the store. Just baby steps away from kleptomania and the clink.

PRO: Kids keep us young, seeing the magic of the world as they discover it for the first time. My boobs may sag, but my spirit will soar.

CON: "Whatever, Trevor!" Yours truly, Broken Twat.

PRO: Spare parts. Max will have someone to borrow organs from. A backup liver. High fives all around!

PRO: Max will have someone to help pick out my casket. And share the weight.

PRO: And he won't be the only one humiliated by his mother's maniacal musings.

Verdict? The jury is out to lunch. A very long lunch. At an all-you-can-eat buffet. And that jury is comprised of everyone who did not win *The Biggest Loser*. Yeah, it's gonna be a while. So next time someone asks me when they can expect the second spawning—you know, so the kids are close together in age—here is my emphatic answer: right now, the only things I'm keeping close together are my legs.

Burn Your Birth Plan
Before It Burns You

You've probably read at least one of the "What to Expect" books: *What to Expect When You're Expecting, What to Expect the First Year, What to Expect During Labour, What to Expect When There's a Human Skull Trapped in Your Pelvis,* etc.

Do these books prepare us for the joys and challenges of motherhood? Or do they just give us a false sense of preparedness for a journey one can't possibly prepare for?

Take my wonderful birthing experience, for starters. (There really should be a sarcasm font.) Did I have a birth plan? Not really. I knew I'd have to play this sucker by ear. I just had one request: drugs, and lots of 'em. Seriously. I was one stretch mark away from making a medic-alert bracelet that read "Stick that Epi in my Dural" for my arrival at the hospital. With a matching necklace, earrings, and anklet that reiterated these instructions. Just so they were 100% clear on where I stood.

Things couldn't have gone more tits up. Nine days overdue, I was induced, and when the Sauce of Satan (aka oxytocin) kicked in, things went from zero to sixty faster than you can say episiotomy. Just a couple hours in, I was begging for narcotics. Epidural, morphine, cocaine—I was not particular about this, nor about having five to ten people staring at my spread eagle that sure wasn't bald.

In waltzes the anesthesiologist—blue-eyed and olive-skinned with a well-endowed medicine cabinet on wheels. My handsome knight in sterilized armour had finally arrived. I gave thanks to the pharmaceutical reps and drug pushers and Snoop Lion and anyone else who had helped make this moment possible.

But my world was suddenly shattered by a cold finger in my cooter and the sound of Nurse Ratched's voice: "Sorry, hun. You're fully dilated. No drugs for you."

Noooooooo. Damn you. Damn every teddy bear on your stupid nurse uniform. Thirty minutes earlier, I had inquired about an epidural, but the Registered (in ill advice) Nurse suggested I hold off because surely it was too early for the mercy of modern medicine, which to me sounded like, "you're being dramatic." So I took her advice and got in the bathtub to seek some relief. I sat in the tub on a stool, buck naked and crying in pain, while my husband, the zookeeper, hosed me down with hot water.

Like a horror scene in slow motion, I watched the anesthesiologist wheel away his wares. He went from hero to zero in the blink of a whispering eye. And that sadistic nurse. A curse on both their houses!

Long story short, I gave birth without so much as an aspirin. I felt everything. EV-REE-THING. That urge to push—wow. Imagine the worst shit cramp possible, then multiply that by ten trash compactors and one supernova. Major G-force in my P-source. Now replace the average medium to large turd with an eight-pound human with elbows, knees, and a head like a honeydew melon. Okay, now eject. Yeah. Ouchy.

As the doctor stitched me up, I kept kicking him out of sheer reflex. Yes, my birth plan was really working out. Give birth Cro-Magnon style? Check! Roundhouse kick the doctor in the throat? Check! So far, so good.

I *thought* I was prepared to bring baby Max home. To the horror of my husband's wallet, I had all the gear. All of it. But Max hated the swing, the sling, and his eight-hundred-dollar crib. I should have kept him in the sock drawer, Benjamin Button style.

I was prepared for the sleepless nights, but I had no idea how difficult it would be to sleep-train a ginger. In the dark of night, I could see his orange wig glowing like fire and brimstone as he howled for hours on end. As soon as he started sleeping through the night, or so I thought, he'd cut a tooth or discover a third lung and resume his vociferous battle with slumber once again.

Nobody prepared me for the Great Boob Catastrophe either. Sure, I knew breastfeeding was going to be draining. But I thought the extra boobage would last, like an eternal token of gratitude from Mother Nature for suckling her latest creation. Clearly, the Great

Mother is more of a lender than a giver because, right after I quit breastfeeding, my rental rack had to be returned to Jumbo Titty-O. Why didn't anyone tell me my girls would wind up looking like golf balls in tube socks? WHY? I went from a nice pre-prego B cup, to a D while breastfeeding, to a post-lactation A. I hadn't worn an A cup since the eighth grade! Not cool. I need at least a B to achieve equilibrium with my ass.

I had all the "What to Expect" books right here. But things kept coming out of left field.

So do these books tell us what to expect? Sure. They give us *some* insight into this scary, unknown world called motherhood. But they leave a lot of things out. They don't warn us that we might not be able to get an epidural if we wait too long. They don't caution us about nurses who think they know our bodies better than we do because they've massaged enough perineum to orbit the earth ten times over. They don't tell us that childbirth is a reenactment of the famous chest-burster[10] scene from *Alien*. And they don't mention that all the cash we spend on baby gear might be better spent on padded bras, stool softeners, and therapy.

But alas, we must remember nothing in life works out exactly as we plan. We have to just go with it. Tuck our ta-tas into our socks and roll with the punches.

At a baby shower for friends of mine expecting twins, there was a little "advice book" on the table where guests were encouraged to leave a few words of wisdom. I kept my note short and sweet: "Now yer fucked."

All About (Blaming) Eve

I hate religion. The whole god thing is so bogus I refuse to capitalize the word. I think I'm a "reluctant atheist" like David Bowie. I want some kind of hope, but my mind just won't let me believe it.

[10] After incubating inside him, the alien baby burst out of John Hurt's chest. Blood spewed in every direction. People were terrified. This is widely considered one of the most disturbing moments in space movie history, second only to John Travolta's tragic decision to star in *Battlefield Earth*.

I totally subscribe to the Creation story, however. Oh yes, that account simply must be true, because in it I find someone (other than my husband) to blame for the heinous experience they call childbirth.

Let's do a little Biblical recap. Six thousand years ago, Eve ate the forbidden fruit in the Garden of Eden, even though god specifically told her not to. Tsk tsk. If it had been a big hunk of Belgian chocolate dangling from that tree, perhaps I could see the error of her ways. But an *apple?* That's just weak, gurlfren.

Her punishment? Well, god took away the X-Box and, to top it off, added this: "I will greatly increase your pains in childbearing.... Your desire will be for your husband, and he will rule over you" (Genesis 3:16).

Thanks a lot there, Female Numero Uno. And thanks a lot to you too, almighty one. It wasn't enough to send her to her tree house?

So mamas and gal pals, we must suffer. It's the legacy we've inherited. From Eve. From Evolution. From Eve-olution. Whatever.

For starters, we must menstruate. The average woman spends about $10,000 on pads and tampons. And don't forget the ibuprofen and chocolate we throw back during shark week. Bloody expensive.

After ninety seconds of unbridled pleasure, we must then carry our subsequent offspring for nine months[11]—a good chunk of our lives—during which time we must endure nausea, swelling, and any number of physical and emotional complications.

Then the fun part—we must squeeze a *human being* into the world through an opening no bigger than the circumference of our husband's "wee one." The "in" door for one head becomes the "out" door for another. Except the exiting head has *two* eyes. And ears. And a big ol' body attached to it. If my husband's widdle guy had been eight pounds and twenty-one inches long (dream on, honey), maybe my emergency exit would have been better prepared for visitors. It's inhumane. Terrorists would list this as "torture technique #7," meaning six other methods of lesser torture would be utilized

---

[11] In nine months, you can grow 4.5 inches of hair and watch the complete *Stars Wars* series 489 times. At the end, you're more like Chewbacca than when you began.

first. Inmates at Guantanamo would not be subject to such cruel and unusual punishment. No, this torture is reserved for the true dregs of society—women.

Then comes the breastfeeding. A task that's exhausting enough (you have to feed every two to three hours, so when are you supposed to find time to sleep, eat, and shop online?), let alone the nipple pain, the plugged milk ducts, the mastitis and thrush and countless other toe-curling boo-boos of the boobies. (See page 30 for more on this colossal suckage.)

"Feed through it," the lactation nurses tell us. Okay, sure, no problem. Give me a shot of whiskey and something to bite down on. An apple maybe?

I won't even get into the incontinence, the scar tissue, the hemorrhoids, and the lifelong struggle with body image. (Yes I will. Keep reading.) And lest we forget the menopause to come and its slew of sucky symptoms that serve to remind us we're drying up like a desert camel's scrotum.

In short, Eve = MC^2. Where MC stands for mommy curse and menstrual cramps and mutilated clitoris.

And don't get me started on the common perception that men get sexier with age while women just get old. How did men get off so easily? All they have to do in this life is shovel snow, lift heavy boxes, put the windshield wash in the car, mow the lawn, and ejaculate. Is this fair? Hell no. Especially when Adam ate the fuckin' fruit too! How was he punished for his defiance? The Bible says god made him "toil for his food from a ground full of thorns and thistles." Whoopdy-freakin-doo. Adam probably made his loyal minion do all the work anyway. He definitely made her harvest his twig and berries.

Eve, and all the women who came after her, got a bum rap. And our bums are not the half of it. Adam got but a slap on the wrist. He should have gotten a smack on the trouser snake. A bag tag at the very least. Where's the justice?

Oh hey, men die first. Sweet. Let's call it even.

Giving Birth:
Cruel and Unusual...Privilege?

My sperm donor and I spent my thirty-first birthday in a prenatal class at the Health Sciences Centre in St. John's. (As it turned out, the class was twice as long as my labour.) We were practicing breathing techniques, and one of the exercises required Andrew and I to turn and face one another. Last time we looked into each other's eyes like this was on our wedding day, about thirty-six weeks and forty pounds ago.

The nurse/instructor told me to breathe—*hee hee* hoooooo—while Andrew leaned toward me and rubbed my shoulders. Without thinking, he said something that permanently etched itself into my memory. The part of my memory where I store reasons to dropkick people in the face and call them "sperm donor" instead of "loving husband." His exact words: "This is going to kill my back."

NO. YOU. DIDN'T. I think even Max cringed in utero. My back had been aching for eight months. Peaceful sleep was a distant dream, and you have to sleep to dream, so I was royally screwed. And the epic pain I was about to endure any day now was going to make the sperminator's backache seem like a hangnail. I was petrified about what was about to happen to me, and he was casually complaining about his back. Not cool, big giant tool.

But despite this slip of the tongue, I'm not bitter. Not toward him, not toward anyone who is exempt from this ungodly pain. I just like to whine about it. It makes me feel better somehow. It's kind of like swearing. I don't really need to curse. But I just like to drop the odd f-bomb now and then to send a little surge of lightning through the ol' bloodstream.

I joke about the nightmarish labour, comparing it to that big, goofy Kool-Aid jug bursting through the brick wall. I tell tales of case-room horror, often employing hyperbole to heighten the entertainment value. It did hurt. A lot. But truth is I'm over it. Well, almost. And I don't really blame anyone for the pain (anymore). Apple-eating Eve is my homegirl. The nurse who told me to hold off on the drugs was doing the best an overconfident meathead can do. And men? How can I resent them? I mean, they're not exactly getting off scot-free. In fact, because they're largely omitted from this unique life experience, I actually feel kind of bad for them.

In every other avenue of life, men and women are equals. (No they're not, but they should be. Just go with it.) We have equal opportunities at work, at school, at play. We may not be able to pee standing up, but we broads can be the best, the boss, the bomb-diggity. Men and women alike, there are no limits to what we can do. The world is our oyster and we both get to shuck the shit out of it.

But this thing—carrying a child and giving birth—men simply cannot do. They will never know what it feels like to bake a person inside of them like a slow-roasted Butterball turkey. They'll never know the exhilaration of having that child, just moments after entering the world, latch onto their breast with sheer animal instinct. Men have nipples, but why? They're as useless as tits on a bull. In fact, they *are* tits on a bull. Men can only sit back and observe the miracle of keeping this spectacular creature alive with nothing more than the nectar of our own bodies.

It sounds too impossible to be true. But god, or evolution, or Aphrodite, or Yoda, or Oprah, or someone, made it very possible. For women and women alone. We may be the subspecies to endure the pain, but we are the lucky ones to have the privilege of this first-hand miraculous life—and life-giving—experience.

So we must have compassion for men, not resentment. And we must do what we can to include them in this experience. In fact, we must enable them to *share* in our pain. We must let them rub our feet, our backs, and our legs. We must permit them to run warm baths for us, paint our toenails, shave our legs, and run out at two in the morning to buy ketchup chips, mangoes, and muffins ("I said *blueberry*, goddamn you! Are you retarded or something?") During labour, we must squeeze their hand so tightly they lose all sensation in their fingers. We must have them fetch the hungry baby from the crib and then put the happy baby back. We must encourage them to spend time with the lil' munchkin, while we go shopping for $300 leather boots. It's the least we can do to include them in this heaven-sent journey from which the cocksuckers have been so unfairly excluded.

Breast Is Best. It Is Also The Worst

Breast is best. Yeah, yeah, yeah, we get it. We believe you. But please don't call breastfeeding "magical," and please stop smiling like that.

A mother's milk may very well be the "perfect food" but the extraction process sure ain't perfect, so let's not pretend. Is it nice to be able to nurture the fruit of your loins with the nectar of your nips? Of course it's nice. It's convenient, even. But it is *not* magical. Unless curling your toes while your vampire baby sucks your nipples four inches down into his throat is magical. And then there's the pressure. I don't mean the pressure to breastfeed (although there is that, big time). I mean *the pressure*. The ratio of force to the area over which that force is distributed. There is a volcano ready to erupt, and that volcano is your tit.

The day Max was born, they told me he could suck away on the ol' bijongas but my milk wouldn't likely "come in" until the following day. They did *not* mean that a nurse would bring me a milkshake. They meant that I would develop a huge, rock-hard uniboob that needed to be relieved or someone would lose an eye—if not by my projectile milk than by my fist. Milk would literally shoot across the room in multiple directions like a sprinkler skitzing out on the lawn.

One way or another, you *must* get the milk out. If the baby is not hungry when you're ready to feed, someone is getting a mouthful of sweater-meat and you don't care who it is. Doctor, nurse, husband, janitor, hospital pastor: I don't care who you are, just get over here and suck on these globes for the love of god.

This rarely happens, of course, because your baby is a voracious glutton. From the moment Max arrived, he was sucking: the world's newest little perv, looking for the nearest nipple. The day we brought him home from the hospital, we caught him trying to suck the shit out of the car-seat. The Boobsey Twins were in for it.

His savage sucking relieved the pressure. But don't get me wrong. It did *not* feel good. It hurt. Like a bitch. But it was the only way to restore some normalcy to my tender torpedoes. I bit my lip and kept my eye on the prize: thirty glorious minutes of feeling relatively normal once my baby aardvark had his fill. (Let's forget about my arseteroids for the moment, and the damage done to Marianas Trench.)

And then the weird sensation of the milk replenishing itself inside me would begin. Just in case I forgot for a second that I was a freakin' *cow*. I could actually feel the milk travelling through my ducts, from some tiny little milk factory deep inside me run by the doozers from Fraggle Rock.

This is a delicate balance between my bongos and my baby. A reciprocity that must go on, 24/7, with no escape but death. We are attached at the tit forever. It will never, ever end. IT CAN'T END. If he decides he's had enough of the twins, I'm screwed. I will have to steal another baby. I will have to pull a Selma Hayek.[12] I will have to slap my lady-lumps into a sandwich press. I will have to sneak into Central Dairies after hours and hook my teats up to the milking machine. When you and your babe are apart, something *must* take his place. Anything. Anyone.

Max was about four months old when I spent the first night ever away from him. Andrew and I went to a wedding about an hour out of town. Conveniently, it was at a hotel, so we booked a room, pumped the milk, bought the wine, and left Max with my mom. It was time for this new mama to par-tay.

Of course, there's no switch on the fun-bags to turn off the milk production, so I'd have to pump at intervals to alleviate the pressure. I packed my trusty breast pump and a couple hundred breast pads and off we went.

An hour or so into the wedding reception, I was practically mooing. Bursting at the seams. It was time to express myself and not in the way Madonna intended. I went up to my room to pump and dump. But the bloody batteries in the pump were dead and I hadn't brought the power cord. KILL ME NOW. Okay wait, don't panic. I retrieved some new batteries from the front desk. Crisis averted.

---

[12] In 2009, Salma Hayek made headlines when she breastfed another woman's baby during a goodwill mission to Sierra Leone. I asked my husband what he thought. He said, "lucky baby."

But the pump still wouldn't work. FUCK YOU, DOUBLE-A ALKALINE ASSHOLES. I had had it with this pumping thing anyway. Max could fill his belly in ten minutes flat but I'd pump for half an hour to get half an ounce of milk. (I eventually posted an ad online and sold the fucker to a guy named Tony.)

Okay. Plan B: manual expression in a hot bath. In other words, milking myself with my own hands like I'm the farmer *and* the cow. The hot bath helps, don't ask me why. I had tried this in the bathtub before out of sheer curiosity and I knew it wasn't an overly effective method, but I had no choice now. It was either do it myself or wander off into the woods to find a baby beaver to latch on, buck teeth and all. I'd leave the wedding every hour or so, run upstairs to our room, whip off my dress, toss my soggy breast pads in the garbage, and jump in a scalding bath to milk myself. Just a shot glass full, but beggars with bursting bazookas can't be choosers. Then I'd jump out of the tub, throw my dress back on, insert two fresh breast pads, and go back downstairs to the wedding. Until I just couldn't take it anymore. Again.

This went on all night. So much for my relaxing evening. This night had gone tits-up. This wedding was dead to me. And don't even bother trying to get frisky later, husband. I'm busy *surviving* over here. Sorry for my lack of romance, but I'm a little occupied with not *exploding*. If I can just make it through the night I will have *all the sex*, I swear.

I thought about leaving. Getting in the car and just driving home. But my husband couldn't drive because he was, of course, drunk on life with his tiny nipples all tucked into his cute little shirt. And I couldn't drive either. I was drop dead tired. All this mammary maintenance had taken its toll. Although, if I did have a car accident, my airbags would cushion the impact. But we'd all drown in breast milk.

We were here for the night. But sleeping was impossible. I had to lie flat on my back because lying on my side, with my side-boob touching the bed, was excruciating. Nobody touch me. Nobody breathe on me. If a feather escapes from the down pillow and lands on my chest, I will surely die. I begged for sleep to overtake me, so when I opened my eyes again I'd be just one hour from seeing my boy with the mouth.

We drove back to town as early as possible the next morning, my back straight against the seat holding on for dear life. Drive, muthafucka, drive. *Oh look, a hitchhiker. And he looks thirsty—pull this fucking milk wagon over!* If a cop had stopped us I would have shot him right in the face; my machine guns were locked and loaded.

And I don't know *what* I would have done if I had a sudden run-in with the breastfeeding Nazis from La Leche League. I was hating this boob-food racket more than ever right now. This didn't just suck tit; it sucked *ass* and *dick* as well. I didn't need anybody getting all up in my jugs with their righteous selves, reminding me how beautiful the bond is between mother and child. Seriously—I know you gals don't have much else to write home about besides your ability to feed a small village with your gigantic, ugly knockers, but please, stick it in yer grandma. I totally agree: breast is best. But just because breast is best does *not* mean we have to love it. I love my son. But I sure didn't love what his birth did to my Snatchbox Twenty. Or how his need to feed turned my tits into ticking timeboobs.

I went on to breastfeed for another six months. But it was a long time before I told anyone about this evening from hell, because the best part of it—the part I thought made the story worth telling—was off limits. Well, I *thought* it was off limits. Turns out my husband doesn't give half as many shits as I thought. So here it comes.

I needn't get into the gory details. Let's just say there was a Plan C. There had to be. Shit was getting primal up in here. I was that guy who got trapped between the rocks for 127 hours and sawed his own arm off. I was one of those rugby players who crashed in the Andes and ate someone's arse to survive. I was up Tit Creek without a paddle. The only survival tool I had left in this Swiss Army Life was my husband. I was truly and unequivocally desperate in this moment. And desperate times call for desperate measures…. Right, honey?[13]

---

[13] Do you really need to ask? Yes. Yes he did.

Children do not care
if their mother is not beautiful.

— ANONYMOUS

CHAPTER TWO

Life Is a Beauty Cuntest

I once watched a show on the Discovery Channel about beauty and what's considered attractive to different cultures around the globe. Even among the most uncivilized tribes, beauty played a role in status. The definitions of beauty differed somewhat, but some attributes were considered universally attractive. Among women: soft skin and a well-proportioned body. Among men: a beating heart.

Female beauty is a big deal. Always was.[1] Look at the ancient Egyptians with their jewel-adorned wigs and lips red with ochre. Look at the Chinese, binding their feet to make them small and dainty. *Who cares that you can't walk, those three-inch footsies are totes fuckable!* Look at portraits from the Renaissance with their flawless skin and silky hair, and the Italian women from that time who used a toxic plant extract to dilate their pupils, which was considered alluring. (Today, it means you're on crack.) Look at the Bible. Sisters Rachel and Leah were both married to Jacob, but no matter

---

[1] Among the 30,000-year-old Chauvet cave paintings, mixed in with the pictures of horses and rhinos, was a "Venus" figure. A vulva painted on a large, overhanging rock pendant that may have been used for worship. I have no idea how this relates to beauty but I can't *not* mention vulva worship.

how many sons "tender-eyed" Leah squirt out of her sin flower, beautiful, barren Rachel was always the favourite.[2]

I mean, beauty is not *everything*. Intelligence and integrity and a willingness to perform fellatio all factor in to your popularity among the penis'd. But there's no denying the importance we place on how we look, and we all subscribe to it, whether we admit it or not. Some people adamantly reject it, but we all know what stick they've been beaten with.

This obsession with beauty rears its ugly, pimply, pale-faced, weak-chinned head more than ever when we become mothers. How much weight we gain during pregnancy. How our babies look at birth. How fast we lose our baby weight, if ever. A great time to really scrutinize the female form, when we only have time to brush *either* our hair *or* our teeth—not both. When the only parts of our bodies getting exercise are our nipples and our right arms thanks to constant baby-bouncing and car-seat curls. Kate Middleton stepped out of the hospital just one day after giving birth to Prince George and within seconds the media exploded with speculation about her weight-loss regimen to get rid of that ghastly post-baby bump. What a bunch of dicks. I mean, she's royalty; *obviously* she's going to be wearing a corset reinforced with whalebone.

In California, I hear women even compare vaginas and get surgery—labiaplasty—to perfect them.

Tiffany: Nice labia majora, girl.

Brianna: Aw thanks. Excellent vulva formation. What are your tits like?

And if you don't surgically perfect the wunder down under, at least you can vajazzle the fuck out of it with crystals and jewels, and don't forget the glue. Because your mediocre muff just ain't sparkly enough. It's also not pink enough, so be sure to pick up a tin of My New Pink Button, a genital cosmetic colourant to restore the "pink" to your dreadfully grey, discoloured vagina. Pussy dye: the last frontier of female imperfection.

---

[2] Jacob only wanted to marry Rachel, but Laban tricked him into marrying his other daughter, Leah. Ha! In yo face, Jacob! That's what you get for thinking with your wang. For more deception, see Genesis 29.

It's one big fuckin' beauty cuntest.

I'm as guilty as the next Barbie wannabe. I lost all my baby weight (other than the half-pound of scar tissue inside my love glove) but I still see myself as an ogre behind a curtain of mascara and miracle mousse. I loathe my water balloony breasts and pay big money for bras that trick people (except my husband—that fucker knows too much) into thinking they're firm and perky. Sometimes I curl my eyelashes for god's sake. How ridiculous is that? If a thief broke in and stole my makeup kit tonight, I'd call in to work ugly.

Ugly Baby Alert: A Face Only a Mother Could Love

So you think you have a cute baby. And maybe you do. It's possible; some of those sneaky C-section babes manage to dodge the ol' cone head.

But come on, new parents, see beyond your baby blinders. Does your newbie look like Steve Buscemi? Would Anne Geddes put your baby way deep in the background?

Oh I forgot. All babies are precious gifts from god. How can they be anything but beautiful? Easily. But I will spare your butt-fugly baby and use my own child to demonstrate.

When Max was born, he was pretty easy on the eyes. Full lips, button nose, and lovely olive skin—Waaaaait a damn second. I quickly recounted all my sexual rendezvi (that's plural for rendezvous) of the last nine months. Hmmm, just one skeety white boy from Mount Pearl; it had to be jaundice. I show people Max's baby album and they ask, "Who's the little Mexican?" I reply, "That's Senor Max. He comes from the village of Taco. It is very hot down there, amigo."

Later, he had such an orange tinge it was as if I'd been impregnated by Ernie. Which could have worked out, come to think of it. I mean—Sesame Street—what better neighbourhood is there to raise your kid in, am I right? If I married Ernie, I could control his every move. Because Ernie is a puppet. A puppet. Get it? But then there's the whole gay thing.

The jaundice went away with the bilirubin and my baby boy was 100% Irish honky. We also stopped calling him Billy Rueben.

But his skin problems did not end there. After a few weeks of cuteness, he started to morph into a kid from the first half of a Clearasil commercial:

Me: So, this is Max. He has a bit of a rash.

Baby Inspector: Aw, what a cute…shirt.

Max was a total gremlin.

Once, I nodded off with him in my arms. Dreaming of my beautiful boy driving a fluffy cloud car with the Care Bears, I woke up and looked down to see his googly eyes and crater face staring back at me. Monsterrrrr! I almost flicked my Schmiegel onto the floor.

But fear not, all you makers of motley munchkins, there is hope. At one month of age, Max looked like a pizza with eyes and hair. But it only lasted a couple of weeks. Today he is god's gift to hobbit women: a full head of copper curls, big brown eyes, a heart-melting smile, and bulging biceps.

But I'm sure there are uglier days to come, at age six or seven, when he starts to lose teeth and grow hair on his shoulders.

I am living proof of the fluctuation of childhood beauty. I was a pretty cute toddler, but my cuteness quotient plummeted in grade school thanks to a few bad hair years and near criminal wardrobe. In my defense, I was not *born* with a Missouri Mudflap.[3] Or those geometrical magic-eye-puzzle jumpsuits. Some kids are born ugly and some have ugly thrust upon them. My pukoid elementary-school days were less the fault of Mother Nature and more the fault of Mother Shirley. Thanks for keeping me humble, Mom. I owe ya. Wait til you see the little number I have in mind for your coffin.

Pobody's Nerfect

What's the first thing you say when you see a newborn baby?

"She's so cute."

"He's so beautiful."

---

[3] A mullet. Or in my case, a femmullet.

"She's got her mommy's nose."

"He's got his daddy's ears. Can you pin them back somehow?" Upon seeing an odd looking baby, a fellow blogger's German wife said, "That baby looks like its mother. Which is not a present." Do we hear how ridiculous we sound? Not just the German. All of us!

I confess. When I was preggers, I was afraid my kid was going to be ugly. Of course, my greatest fear was that he would be born with a debilitating disease. But my second greatest fear was that he would have the map of Lake Michigan (which looks like a dick) on his face or a head shaped like Stewie's on *The Family Guy* or satellite dish ears (free cable would be little consolation). Everybody hopes for a beautiful child. It's only natural, especially given the skin-deep world in which we live.

We want our kids to be lovely and not just because we want to marvel at them and go "aww." We want them to be attractive to spare them the ridicule that comes with *not* being attractive. Freckle face, fatso, dork, four-eyes, beanpole, short stuff—kids can be very cruel. And creative! My childhood nicknames? Carrot-top. Big Red. And the real kick in the freckles: Rubberhead.[4] We'll do whatever we can to protect our kids from that pain. Trouble is, helping them conform to the ideals of beauty to evade rejection only perpetuates the problem.

I pick up a magazine and flip through the pages of women looking impossibly perfect, and I come to three conclusions: (1) Wow, those women are flawless, (2) Fuck, I'm hideous, and (3) I'm so glad I have a boy.

For some reason, guys can be pudgy, hairy, and imperfect. If they're charming, funny, or smart, they can snag and shag the cutest girl in the room. Throw in a guitar and a trust fund and he's a red-hot commodity. Seriously, count the mediocre if not motley crew of rock stars that have married supermodels. But the chubby girl with the moustache? She can play the piano *and* the harp while doing stand-up comedy and juggling fire; hope she likes black and white

---

4 My surname was Combden, which evolved into Condom, which morphed into Rubberhead. It didn't help that my best friend's surname was Harding. (Pause.) Yeah. Exactly.

and gambling with Cheerios[5] because she may as well sign up for the convent now. Well, unless she sucks a mean Lake Michigan. Could be a game changer.

Seriously, these supermodel supreme beings represent an ideal that 99.9% of us can't possibly achieve. They are genetically predisposed to thinness and sky-high cheekbones. The vast majority of us—no matter how much we exercise and diet and groom—will simply never look like this; it's just not in our DNA. And yet this unattainable imagery is presented to us—and our impressionable children—every single day on TV, on the Internet, in magazines, on larger-than-life billboards. We are so immersed, we don't even realize the damage it inflicts. Even these models can't achieve the perfection they represent. Virtually all of them are airbrushed into oblivion. I work in the art room of an ad agency; I've witnessed the wonders of Photoshop. Even Cindy Crawford once said, "I wish I looked like Cindy Crawford." As if her supermodel self were not a lofty enough standard to strive for, they shave a little off her thighs and magically erase the blemishes from her skin. Except for THE MOLE,[6] of course. "Don't touch the mole. Actually, yes, make the mole rounder and smoother looking, okay thanks. There, that's better. Now, little girls, here's what beautiful looks like. Good luck with that." And the little girl looks in the mirror and sees a dozen things she wants to change before she can be happy.

I was an ugly child. Buck teeth, freckles, pasty white, rail thin, and red hair sculpted into a Kentucky Waterfall. Did you just conjure up the biggest hillbilly imaginable? My third-grade picture is like a screen capture from *The Hills Have Eyes*. When other little girls my age were swinging pigtails like Punky Brewster, I looked like the love child of Raggedy-Ann and Dog the Bounty Hunter. My personal slogan: business in the front, party in the back. It's not a pretty picture, let me tell you. But thankfully, for most of my childhood, I didn't know I was ugly; I was just me. Playing with my

---

[5] Because gambling with money is the work of Satan and god eats Cheerios for breakfast.

[6] Cindy Crawford's mole is the second most masturbated over beauty mark in the history of blemishes, second only to Marilyn Monroe's. We call this practice self-*mole*station.

Barbie, I was oblivious to her universal status as the ultimate blonde bombshell; the epitome of female beauty. The women around me were not weight-obsessed. Nan wore a moo-moo and chewed on the salt-beef bone. Mom never wore a speck of makeup; I wore lipstick sometimes, but only because it tasted like strawberries. I had no prissy older sister to idolize, just a brother who kicked my ass at *Jeopardy* and taught me how to catch. My dad wore mismatched clothes, sometimes backwards (true story); he was as far away from vanity as humanly possible. Nobody ever told me I was beautiful, and nobody ever told me I was ugly. Maybe the mullet rendered people speechless. Or maybe I was valued for humour, intelligence, and honesty; maybe that's the long (on the back) and the short (on the front) of it.

But inevitably, adolescence happened and opened my eyes to the female ideal that I clearly did not represent. I suddenly became aware of my particular weight issue—I was too skinny! The actresses on television were thin, but they were shapely, womanly, sexy thin. Unlike Blair on *The Facts of Life*, I was a piece of two-by-four with fly-bites for boobs, wearing long-johns inside my jeans in a pathetic attempt to look more like an hourglass and less like a human erection. Mom and her friend Sophie poked fun at me, cautioning me not to run up the stairs too fast with my gigantic jugs: "You might get two black eyes!" Laugh it up, ladies-of-large-fun-bags. To a ten-year-old girl, that stings. And clearly, it sticks in the memory, forever deeming me, at least a little, that insecure little girl.

I turned out okay, stronger and wiser for the experience. But I can see how some girls end up down a bad, bad path. Girls who idolize Britney Spears and her bare midriff, who look up to calorie-counting parental figures who remind them to lay off the cookies. Not because cookies are unhealthy, but because they make you fat, and nobody wants a fat girl except the dudes in Mauritania![7] What does that do to a young mind? The mind of a girl who's just trying to find herself in the first place? She finds herself not good enough,

---

[7] In the West African country of Mauritania, girls are force-fed camels' milk by the gallons to reach the aesthetic ideal: obesity. It'd be a great spot to open a Moo-Moos Ice Cream. You know, if the people weren't dirt poor.

forever pursuing a goal she can never reach. I hear about girls with anorexia, turned into something they never intended to be, trapped in a house of mirrors—in none of which they see their true selves. How do they escape that skewed perception? How do they reprogram their brains? There is no prescription for perfection. There is no perfection.

I'm so thankful my child is a boy. But I know he's not entirely exempt from it all.[8] One day, he'll probably be choosing to spend his life with one of these creatures. Hopefully one that's not checking herself in every mirror, puddle, and silver spoon. And while he may dodge society's demands for beauty with his boyish charms, he won't escape society's expectation of those "boyish charms," the rules of masculinity he's supposed to live up to. Boy or girl, I need to teach my child what's truly important. But saying "real beauty is on the inside" just doesn't cut it. There is just too much *stuff* working against those puny words. Everywhere you look, it's there. Beautiful people on every surface. On the bus shelter while you're waiting for the bus. On the bus itself as it stops to let you on. On the walls and ceilings and seats inside the bus. On street billboards as the bus drives past. On the iPhone in your hand while you're waiting for your YouTube video to play while riding…you guessed it…the bus. Beauty is always up in your face. You know, that face that could use some expensive cream, cosmetics, and surgery. Dove's Real Beauty campaign can only do so much.

Thing is, I make that *stuff.* I peddle the beauty myth. I use it to sell shit, by making people uncomfortable with what they have (or don't have) and lust for something more. Ads constantly create desire for fictions we can't actually live. If we could, we'd just live that shit and stop buying more stuff, wouldn't we?

Maybe this makes me a ball of contradiction. But maybe it also makes me well-equipped to teach Max the difference. Filter the images he sees. Tell him the tricks. Show him Oprah in real life, and then Oprah after hours of make-up, dramatic lighting, perfect camera angling, and award-winning Photoshop—all after a shopping

---

8 For more of this gender bullshit, see page 96.

MotherFumbleR

spree at the Spanx store, of course. Help him develop the tools to see beneath the façade, to keep it real in a plastic world.

I just want him to resist the myths, not eschew all things beautiful. It's okay to be beautiful and like beautiful things. One day, Max will probably fall in love with a pretty girl. And why not? As long as she's not *just* pretty. Pretty girls can get a raw deal too. "Oh, she's too pretty to be smart or funny or talented." That's just not true.

It's not that advertising is inherently bad either. It's not all gorgeous models all the time. It's not all shiny cars and sparkling diamonds and crap to keep up with the Joneses. I recently created a campaign using photography of real-life dairy farmers to help a client sell milk. The ads were beautiful and retouched to perfection, but the farmers were real, the milk was good, and the only breasts in the ads belonged to the cows.

Advertising is powerful. It can create a material world obsessed with thinness and glamour. And it can create real, positive change in the world with social campaigns that compel people to stop smoking, read to their kids, report domestic violence, donate to children's hospitals, and treat animals right. Sometimes it even sells you products you really do need, like ointment for your bum grapes.

In spite of the harm some advertising does, I'm in the best place I can be: *on the inside.* You know, with the other handful of female creative directors surrounded by dicks and balls, though women control 80% of consumer spending. We can't change the superficial desires of the world, but maybe we can create some kind of tiny but important shift. Our job is to deliver results for our clients (or we'll have to run along and become nurses and kindergarten teachers like normal women), but maybe there's a way to achieve those results in a way that'll mess with our kids' heads a little less. If the essence of creativity is making something new, surely using a skin-and-bone supermodel is not the only way to sell a pair of jeans. Maybe I'm wrong. Maybe reality is not enough. I don't know. But I can damn well try and find out. I can do my part on the inside, and help Max translate it all from the outside.

Of course, this is a constant battle full of paradox and contradiction and sudden urges to punch myself square in the face. I can teach Max to resist the beauty myth, but if I'm falling victim to it myself…what the fuck? One morning as I stood in the bathroom mirror engrossed in my usual routine, Max startled me: "What you doing, Mommy?" He was standing in the doorway, god knows for how long. I was doing the worst thing possible—curling my eyelashes. Fuck. There's no good answer to this question. Curling my eyelashes? I may as well say, "stuffing anal beads into my lower bowel," that's how shameful curling my eyelashes feels. I would have preferred he ask me where babies come from. At least the answer to that one is just "vaginas" and not "because Mommy is a superficial dick who wants people to dream about banging her meat sleeve through her eyelashes." I eventually arrived at the next-best thing to a good answer: "I'm making sure my lashes are swept away from my eyes so I can see how beautiful the world is now that you're in it." But it came to me about six months too late. I've tucked it away for the next episode of *Are You Smarter Than a Three-Year-Old?*

Get in the Goddamn Pool

I used to look pretty good in a swimsuit.

I've always had a glorious booty. But now, it's just not that bootiful. Not without fabric wrapped tautly around it, deceptively squishing it all together. One of the great discoveries of my thirties: I look way better in clothes.

Now don't get me wrong, the lovely lady landscape has not changed that much, even after gaining forty pounds and producing an eight-pound baby. "You haven't changed *that* much, babe," says the husband, confirming that I have indeed changed. Asshole.

Where'd the other thirty-two pounds of baby bubble wrap go? I'll attribute three or four pounds to the placenta, which Andrew took a picture of and showed me just moments after giving birth. Thanks for that, honey. I had endured the most unimaginable pain to produce a ground-beef pillow sham. So proud.

Most of the chubs evaporated with my breast milk; Max sucked it out of me like a rabid wolverine pup. And the rest of it—just a handful—went to that place where my ass says hello to my thighs, which we'll call Hammityville. (People who dare to tread there are terrorized by the ghost of a scary, saber-toothed pig.)

Now all you meatier mamas out there, don't be hatin'. Even when you're a small person, the shift in certain anatomical areas can be traumatic. And that's just what this is: a shift. Some places inward, some places outward, all places downward. It's certainly not the hard body of my twenty-three-year-old self. It's an increasingly mushy mass of lard clinging to an exhausted, hunched-over skeleton.

October. Not a great time to buy a swimsuit, but that's exactly what I was shopping for. Summer was done like dinner, but I intended to keep Max swimming regularly at the pool. I'm not into the Mom Jeans look, but I needed a swimsuit that was a little more mother and a little less stripper. Going to the local pool with my toddler in December in a hot-pink push-up bikini top and a string bikini bottom with a palm tree on the butt just seems a little silly now. I once vowed to never utter these words, but…I needed a one-piece. (*Psycho* theme music up.)

So I skipped off to Sportchek to try on swimsuits. (I'm a sporty thirty-something; I don't need to shop for a swimsuit at freakin' Tan Jay, okay?) As expected, there were slim pickins: ironic wording when you're looking for something that will make you look slim, which none of these did. Who designed these things? Gumby's mom? Where do I shove my goods? Into my belly button? Hmm, this one's not so bad, I think. Amazing how Lycra can flatten out your tummy and thrust your excess ass flab out into the world! It reminded me of when my grandmother used to bake bread. She'd mix and knead the dough and leave it to rise in a big bowl on the kitchen table, covered in a dishcloth. Many hours later the dough would spill out over the sides of the bowl. Her expanding buns of sticky dough could not be contained. Likewise, this swimsuit couldn't contain my gelatinous buns of juicy ginger heiny. The white meat poofed out from around the elastic a little too offensively for my liking. If the elastic were a little less, well, elasticy, all would be well. But something's gotta give. There wasn't enough fabric here to make a doily.

And for some added perspective, the lighting in the change room was designed to help you look tanned, and the mirror was clearly bought from a circus liquidation sale—one of those skinny trick mirrors. (Soon enough I'll be seeing the bearded lady staring back at me.) If not for this trickery, I'd probably have been in there slitting my wrists with my car keys.

And Sportchek would never sell a swimsuit! When I went into the change room, I joked to the young male attendant, "I'll probably be coming out of here very angry."

"You all do," he replied, deadpan.

Imagine the self-loathing this young man has witnessed. No woman is ever completely satisfied with herself. We are idiots and can't even help it.

This idiot's problem: I need a medium to large bottom and a small top. One-piece suits just don't come that way. Otherwise they'd use triangles as mannequins.

I have junk in the trunk and nothing on the roof rack. What little was up on the roof has been stored in the trunk. My husband can't even fit his golf clubs back there now. Not even his putter. Not even his balls.

Come to think of it, I've always wondered why my husband, a self-declared "breast man," ever chose yours truly of bitty boobs and ample badonkadonk. (Oh come on, you know I chose him, but you get the point.)

So I bought the one-piece suit that fit my top half, because I can't have my wobbly, deflated water balloons slipping out of my armpit holes. Which means the bottom half of the suit is a bit too small, and Nan's loaf is assaulting the world around it from all sides. FUCK IT.

Here is my theory. I am thirty-five years old. This is nature's way of preparing me for what is to come. A little bit of cellulite here, an extra fold of skin there. Am I thrilled about it? Hells no. But I accept it because, hey, it could be worse. And it will be. Check back in ten years.

Besides, I have distractingly fabulous hair on my side. Sure my posterior is bigger, but I can make my *hair* bigger to divert the eyes. If I combed my hair out with a brush, you'd mistake me for one of the Pyramids of Egypt. And who wants to look at someone's flabby ass when there's a wonder of the fuckin' world before their very eyes? Exactly.

I imagine myself in thirty or forty years, old and crusty and decrepit. But from behind and fully clothed, all you see are my flowing strands of golden hair. Onlookers expect a young Celtic goddess to be on the other side of that magical mane. Like the scarlet-haired heroine from *Brave*, perhaps. But I whirl around—in slow motion, of course—and reveal the face of…Mama. The one they throw from the train.

Maybe I'll let the hair go grey to soften the blow. But I don't know…long, flowing *grey* hair is more like a smoke trail than an asset. A smoke trail, because the fire down below is now the smoldering remains of a burning bush.

It's a gradual decline into fugliness, and thank the baby Jesus. Think about it. If you were a hot-as-balls sex goddess, went to bed, and woke up looking like Bea Arthur, you'd learn to tie a noose before breakfast. Life isn't photographed in time-lapse. The aging process is measured, and this way we accept our downward spiral a bit at a time, and nobody needs to get their knickers (or their neck) in a knot.

Just let it go, ladies. Do what you can to stay the best you can be, but don't be crazy cakes about it. Is it really that important that you look like you're nineteen in a two-piece? (Especially those of you in my neck of the woods where summer is but a fleeting glimpse and one swimsuit could last a lifetime.)

Perfection is unattainable, especially as we get older, which we *all* are getting, by the way, no matter how much Oil of Olay[9] we're bathing in. Those nineteen year olds are just a couple steps behind us; we all face the same fate, we're just on different timelines.

There's no denying it. Youth is *typically* more physically beautiful. It's not right or fair, but it's true. That's what people like to see, so

---

[9] They actually call it Olay now. Just Olay. Because Oil is the devil.

MotherFumbler

47

naturally that's what they're shown: fresh faces and bodacious bods. Even when marketing to an older demographic, we use younger models, because that's how older folks sees themselves. My boss once attended research groups throughout the US for a campaign he was developing for an online pharmacy. His layouts showed pictures of people fifty-five to seventy years old, with grey hair and wrinkles. Every one of the participants said the website wasn't for them. "I'm not that old," they said. They were the same age as the people in the layouts.

Advertising just picks up where evolution leaves off, really. We are at our finest and most physically attractive when we are most fertile. It's survival of the fittest thighs up in here.

But come on. Darwin Schmarwin. We all know beauty is a much more complex, intangible thing than straight teeth and a small waist. Or maybe this wisdom only comes with age. Remember what you were like at twenty? I do. My twenty-four-inch waistline was about the only thing I was certain of. Everything else was questionable. Life was a big WTF, although WTF hadn't even been invented yet so it was more like a Hilroy scribbler full of question marks in neon highlighters and sparkle pens. I was a wreck. Most twenty year olds are. I'd never go back. Not even for those abs.

Beauty is a balance. And I don't mean of tits and ass. I'm talking about confidence and self-respect and knowing who you are. It's a light in the eyes, but its source is on the inside. And not even the most stunning set of peepers can fake it.

Youth does not equal beauty. Sure, there is twenty-something beauty. Lots of it. But there is also thirty-something beauty. And forty-something beauty. And fifty-something beauty. And so on, right up til your big, beautiful death. You can't compare your beauty to a younger generation. You just can't. There are too many variables at play. And forget about competing, missus. We are all on the same team.[10] Try not to shoot lasers at the young thing your husband is undressing with his big, stupid eyes. The penis'd one is a weak, primitive creature. Hold your beautiful head high. Feel the

[10] The V-Team. V is for vagina. And victory.

light behind your eyes. Do that young woman proud because soon she'll be right there where you are now. Show her there's a whole lot of awesome to look forward to yet.

Listen up, all you mothers whose bodies will never, ever be quite the same. Take care of your goods for the sake of your health and your self-esteem, but take your flaws in stride. Remember, you made something beautiful. A person. A motherfuckin' person! And that makes you a thing of beauty. Even if your vagina looks like a dropped pie.

Surely by now you've had enough loved ones bite the big one to know life is short. In the grand scheme of things, which ends in your imminent death, who gives a motherfuck that you look like you're wearing an inner tube *inside* your swimsuit? Seriously. Work with what you got. Wear that dress. Shake that ass. Get in the goddamn pool and play with your kids. Throw open a window and fuck the night. I don't even know what that means, but do it. Because guess what—in ten or twenty years when things are worse for wear, you'll look back at your former self and say, "damn, I wasn't so bad." You will hate yourself, not because of how you look but because of what a self-loathing douchebag you were back then. Don't let the cellulite go to your head. Better to have it on your sweet ass.

Like Mother, Like Son of a Gun

Max looks like me. It's only fair. I did all the work to get him here. What did my husband do? Spray his seed, big whoop. Anyone with a working hose could have done that.

I actually want Max to look like his dad so Andrew will feel proud. And also so he'll know I wasn't a dirty slut. I mean does he really *know* that I wasn't? I can profess that I only slept with him, but there's no way to prove it without a DNA test. Some people say Max is just like Andrew. No doubt, seeing physical features in the child that mirror the man goes a long way in proving a kid's paternity, but not *all the way* if daddy has a handsome, hung brother.

Or two.[11] But even Andrew doesn't see it. He thinks they're all nuts. Speaking of nuts, that's about the only thing my husband and son have in common.

People see what they want to see. On at least two separate occasions, I've remarked on how much a kid looks like his or her mom or dad, only to find out the kid was freakin' adopted.[12] Open mouth, insert foot. Make that *feet*. On another occasion I noted the uncanny resemblance of a little girl to her father, only to discover later that the dude was completely sterile. I tried to imagine what her biological father might look like, but when I closed my eyes all I could see was a sweaty guy jerking into a cup surrounded by sticky magazines.

Maybe different people just see different things. Certain features stand out to one person more than they do to another. Max's hair and gingerliciousness are the first things most people see, hence the likeness to me. But some people go right to the brows. The Murphy caterpillars of the Amazon Rainforest. I do not have those. Not on my forehead anyway.

Who knows who Max will resemble in time? Nobody. Maybe he will look like his Poppy Jim—prominent Fogo Island nose, strong teeth, and no ass; Dad had just enough ass to shit from.

Genetics. What an amazing thing. It's immortality as character and features endure through the ages. I have two sister friends who were born with "apricot ears" like their father. All growing up, they were self-conscious about their furry, folded-over little ears, always covering them up with their hair. Their dad died in a car accident when they were just five and ten. So when Tracey gave birth to her first baby girl and saw the little ears on the sides of her head, I am not sure if she felt mortified or happy. I know how I felt. What an awesome thing. Amber, who will never know her grandfather, has at least one little piece of him. Better to hear him with, my dear.

Admittedly, this story would not be as sweet if, instead of apricot ears, we were talking about a giant, hairy goiter.

---

[11] You're welcome, brothers-in-law Chris Murphy and Geoff Murphy.
[12] Conversely, on one occasion I assumed a white woman's Asian daughter was adopted. All little Asian girls are adopted, aren't they? Not the ones whose moms mate with Korean guys, apparently.

This Is Epic

The great poet Steve Tyler of Aerosmith (as well as some dead dude named Ralph Waldo Emerson) once said, "Life is a journey, not a destination."

Word. If I've learned anything about motherhood so far (other than that physically becoming one hurts like a bitch) it's: *I have no idea where this is going.* I mean, I think I'm on a path that will take me somewhere good with a happy, healthy child and enough sanity to live out the remainder of my days not randomly handing out wedgies at the mall. But I can't be certain. Destination: unknown. So, by simple deduction, all I really have is this journey.[13] (Thanks, Steve and Ralph, for narrowing down my entire human existence to two things.)

But I used to think this journey had to be epic. Like the trek from your bedroom to the bathroom in the middle of the night except the exact fucking opposite. I mean, think about the word: *journey.* Like Frodo and Sam's epic adventure through Middle-Earth. Like Odysseus's epic voyage home after the fall of Troy. Like Marty McFly's epic journey into the past where he gets groped by his own mom (EPIC EW). I mean, if life is a journey and it's the only one we get, then we must live large, right? We must pursue greatness, seek breathtaking beauty, and create monumental moments with an instrumental soundtrack by Enya playing in the background. And, of course, capture it all on camera so they'll have proof that *"epic life"* really should be carved into your headstone after your *epic death.*

It's a tall order. Most nights I don't go to bed thinking, "What an epic day that was." I go to bed thinking, "Well I'm glad that's over." Actually, I sometimes yell "Success!" at the top of my lungs (and in a Kazakstanian accent)—not because it was a magnanimous day for the record books, but because everyone in my immediate care is still breathing.

Every potentially epic journey goes to pot. Even the simplest

---

[13] This is actually terrible logic. I'm assuming there are only two things: the journey and the destination. Maybe there is something else, like rocking back and forth in the fetal position, for example.

endeavour usually turns into a supreme shit-show, performed by the Shit Sisters from Shitville.

There's this path near our house called the Gallows Cove Trail. It's the kind of ocean-side path you see in magazines, and it's right here in our backyard's backyard. If all the homes between our house and this trail were to mysteriously burn down, we'd have a majestic view of the Atlantic Ocean. And a whole lot of explaining to do. Hard to believe that, just ten kilometres that-a-way (see my finger pointing?), there's a Walmart full of people buying toilet paper and chicken fingers. In New York or Toronto or Montreal or even Halifax, you'd have to drive many miles from the city centre to find this kind of natural majesty. It's stunning. It's *epic*. But even here, shit happens.

The very name of the place should be a hint: The Gallows[14] Cove Trail. Hmmm. Somebody's *probably* going to get maimed. Conveniently connected to the Gallows Cove Trail are the Disembowelment Path and the Breast Ripper[15] Roadway. If you lose your way, no sweat—there will be a trail of blood you can follow back to civilization.

One Sunday morning, I hit the trail with Turbo Ginger and Splash the Portuguese water dog who, if given the choice between a floating hamburger and a drowning you, would certainly choose the meat. But damn she's cute. We linked onto the trail near the house, so the first leg of our journey was downhill. Which quickly became a metaphor. I let both boy and dog out of my grasp once we got past the jagged cliffs where Turbo Ginger could fall and ginger snap in half. We were safe on the trail now, protected by an old rickety fence lashed with rusty barbed wire. (A few facial lacerations beats full-body shark bait.)

It was a beautiful morning. The kind of morning you see in orange juice and Viagra commercials. Splash did her usual *Braveheart* routine, galloping ahead and circling back repeatedly, relishing the

---

[14] Gallows: a structure, typically of two uprights and a crosspiece, for the hanging of criminals.

[15] Breast Ripper: a medieval torture device reserved for women. Use your imagination. Actually, don't.

fresh air and freedom. Max lumbered alongside in his favourite rubber boots, traversing rocks, small streams, and fallen branches.

But the rubber boots, while cute, were not a wise footwear choice for a bumpy path. A fuck-tard mommy move indeed. And I'd soon pay for it. Ten minutes in, Turbo Ginger was begging to be carried. And then he wanted his boots off altogether. So I carried everything: backpack, boots, dog leash, and thirty-pound human, all the while trying to take photos—obviously a top priority at times like these.

I was sweating like a hooker during a sermon, lugging this load and threatening the dog not to stray too far off; there was no way I could work the leash too. Eventually Max was ready to get back on his feet, so I leaned forward and gently slid him down into the soft grass that skirted the trail. I threw the camera down nearby and proceeded to put his boots back on his feet. *Swoomp!* The distinct sound of teeth on metal. Splash had snatched up the camera. Four-letter-words echoed from the headlands.

"You furry little fucker, get back here or I'll turn you into a bath mat!"

She was very obedient. I had played the dreaded bath mat card. She came running right back to me. Without the camera. I scoured the grass and surroundings for it, all the while threatening both Splash and Max not to go far. But Max was already running full tilt, his feet clearly rejuvenated.

I found the camera lying near the trail, bathed in slobber but intact, and I ran to catch up to my Mini Pooper. Yes, that's what I said. When I caught up to him, he was squatting—and not because he was looking at rocks. What's that sound? A moose grunting in the trees? Nope, just my kid's vociferous arse and its toxic emissions. But there'd be no diaper-changing out here, no sir. He'd just have to take that shit home with him. Somehow I knew he wouldn't mind; getting his diaper changed when he's having fun is a fate worse than death.

Good thing, because it was going to be a long walk home; he had to bend down to pick up every effin' rock along the way. A rock in his left, a rock in his right: double-fisted. Oh, but then he sees another one that he wants. But he only has two hands. Hmmm, one's gotta go. He thinks for a second, throws one down, picks up the new one, and we're moving on. Until he sees another rock. And the trading-up continues. He'll be doing this with women one day, if he's lucky. Hopefully not when he's toting a chocolate log in his shorts. Chicks don't dig dat. But I sure hope he has better taste in the ladies. Nevermind the smooth, coloured, unique rocks. Max likes the ones you find after a construction company has done blasting—the sharp, dull, grey ones covered in dust. The ones that poke holes in your pockets like ninja death stars.

My wannabe-epic excursion was on its way to *epic fail*. Yet another day that started out as a triumphant adventure, then flipped into a desperate struggle to survive. But then something clicked. I surrendered my pursuit of anything resembling perfection and just opened my eyes. I looked—like, *really* looked—at Max. He wasn't looking with wonder at the big blue sky or the deep blue sea. He was fascinated by what was within his reach and underfoot: snappy twigs and squishy muck, pointy rocks and low-hanging dogberries. The things I only look at to avoid getting my boots dirty. The things I step on only to get a better view of the epic vista I'm about to capture with my Digital SLR. Max doesn't give a damn about epic, not even the epic turd rolling around in his Huggie.

I blame advertising. I work in a world of perfect words atop perfect pictures, where everything is super fast and super sexy and super super. I have to retrain my brain to slow down and see what's right in front of me. Trees, some dead and beautifully twisted. Some were even twirled up together as if they refused to let the wind tear them apart. Birds flickered from twig to twig, some crossing the trail fast and low to the ground like they were trying to trip us. Squirrels chittered over here, then over there, passing secret messages from one end of the forest to the other: *The stupid humans are coming, the stupid humans are coming*. I could hear the ocean cheering us on. But I didn't need to take a picture. It was music, so I just listened. I guess there is magic in this small stuff. Max can see it so much better than I because he's smaller and—let's face it—smarter.

And Max is totally right to like these rocks. They're not ugly; they're ancient. This was no ordinary rock in his grubby hand; this was a prehistoric piece of the universe. This rock was here before the dinosaurs. It has always been here. A beauty that cannot be destroyed. How fragile we are by comparison. How temporary. We are all on our way to the gallows, baby. *That* is the only destination of which we can be sure.

The most beautiful thing on this trail became clear to me, and it had shit in its shorts. My muddy-faced, wide-eyed explorer was enjoying his journey, finding his way, showing me that the most awesome things are close up. Not just in my backyard, but holding my hand. They're so close up, we look right past them, searching for something greater, something perfect, something epic. Which makes life less like a journey and more like a series of destinations you never quite reach. It's not the big moments at all. It's all the in-between stuff. That's where the beauty is. That is the epic journey. And if we don't pay attention, we'll miss it.

Hey, Mother, I come bearing a gift.
I'll give you a hint. It's in my diaper
and it's not a toaster.

— STEWIE, *THE FAMILY GUY*

CHAPTER THREE

Welcome to Smotherhood

Ah yes, the clutch purse: how I miss thee. I remember leaving the house carrying everything I needed in a handbag the size of an envelope. Lip gloss, tampon, money, emergency pantyhose, emergency mints, emergency condom (now you're going way back), emergency mace. Everything I needed to take on the world was right here in the palm of my hand.

Now I'm carrying Sir Edmund Hillary's backpack of provisions, and none of it is for me (other than the ice axe). In the first couple of years, I lugged around burp cloths for spit, diapers for shit, extra baby clothes in case the burp cloths and diapers didn't do their jobs, and a hundred other things to facilitate the survival and cleanliness of this doughy little person.

Oh wait, there's something in here that's not for Max. Check out the stack of breast pads for my leaky boobs. You know, those spongy circles I buy in bulk that I notice peek-a-booing out of my V-neck shirt *after* I've gone through the checkout line at the grocery store. Yes, those are for me. Thanks, Me. You shouldn't have. No really. No really.

And don't forget the other pads I toted around for the first few weeks while the crime scene in my underwear was still under investigation. Each one could have doubled as a travel pillow.

This ain't no purse. It's a goddamn plumbing repair kit. So long, stylish leather clutch. I guess you've gone to live with the spontaneous hikes and weeknight movies and lazy days in bed.

Time Waits for No Mom

I hate clocks. It's either too late or too early. There's either not enough time or too much time. And clocks have three hands. That's just not fair. I want to punch a baby.

I was in labour for three hours: not enough time. Yes, that's what I said. There's a reason you dilate slowly: to stretch your Screwez Canal gradually, to ready it for the emergence of the M.V. Homo Sapien.

I pushed for forty minutes: too long. I have heard of women pushing for two to three hours, which is just plain madness. After more than an hour of that ungodly pain, I'd be jabbing the nurse's utility scissors straight into my husband's chest. Come on, he's at the hospital. He'd be totally fine.

I spent six days in the hospital: too long. By day two, everyone thinks you're home with your baby going "coo-chi-coo, coo-chi-coo," when you're actually in the hospital crying. Just crying.

I fed Max every two to three hours for ten to fifteen minutes: too often. And too quick. Max was such an aggressive sucker. When he was done I'd have to push my nipples back in about six inches. I swear he could suck the circuit-breakers off a cyborg.

All this by-the-clockiness, and I don't even wear a watch.

Motherhood was a wake-up call via an old-school alarm clock that clangs and quakes right there on the nightstand, but you can never reach to turn it off because, unlike the clock, you only have two hands, and there's a baby in one and a bottle of vodka in the other.

Truth is, there's no getting along for me and this Father Time fucker. When I was on maternity leave, I'd go days on end without showering, eating nothing but muffins. I used to wonder what mothers did on mat leave with all that…that *time*! Then I got on the mother bus and Max took me to school. He consumed me—my time, my social life, my sweater meat. Every three days, I'd look in the mirror, pick the blueberries out of my teeth, and scrape the puke off my shirt. MILF? Yeah, if the F stands for Flog.

Now that I'm back at work, there's a different kind of timelessness. I get up, wrestle with Max and our ginger afros to get us both ready for the day, drop him off at daycare, and get to work right on time. And by "right on time," I mean ten minutes late. I work all morning, buy pull-ups and food at lunchtime, go back to work for the afternoon, and get home in time to feed, bathe, and tuck the boy into bed, with some love jammed in there somewhere.

Then I look at the husband. Nope. No time for that tomfoolery. I have bills to pay, work to finish, and sheep to count.

On the other hand, when you're home with the kids with no escape other than death, there is a little too much time. Admit it. It's barely noon and you're already asking for the sweet release of bedtime. We know we shouldn't wish our time away. Life is short. We're fully aware that in fifteen or twenty years, our hearts will ache for these days of choo choo trains and applesauce. And yet we urge time onward because, in spite of our superhuman, multi-tasking maternal skills, we are human.

A Work(ing Mother) in Progress

To work or not to work? That is the question—for those mothers who have the choice. The only choice I have is which shirt will I wear today? Ah yes, this one. The only one without baby graffiti on it. Excellent.

These days, it's extremely difficult for the average family to survive on a single income. As much as I want to believe all you need is love, John Lennon, my empty fridge suggests otherwise. You may say I'm a dreamer, but I can't help but add a few things to the list of necessities: clothes, shelter, food, and a reservoir of homogenized milk.

Should mothers go back to work or stay home and raise their children? Who the hell knows? Some women think putting children in daycare is next to abandonment. I do see the absurdity of bringing a child into the world and then handing him or her over to someone else to raise eight to twelve hours a day. I also know women who have returned to work after a second or even third child, even though the cost of childcare devours their entire paycheck. A reasonable price for sanity, I guess. Or often, it's about keeping a good job you'll want to return to when the kids finally stop invading your country and go off to school. Sometimes it's even about staying in the game, just in case one day you find yourself back in Singleville with a resumé last updated on a floppy disk. Sounds cynical, but Stats Canada doesn't pull the 40% divorce rate out of a bingo machine.

Both choices are difficult. Both entail some sort of sacrifice. And both have their benefits and their bummers. My year of maternity leave opened my weary eyes to the fact that full-time motherhood is kookily consuming. When I returned to work, I would regularly proclaim my admiration for stay-at-home moms.

"You have the tough job," I'd declare, meaning well.

But one day, my friend Kelly put me in my place with one short response. A mother of four boys, including seven-year-old twins, she simply said, "It might be hard for you, but it's not for me."

Snap! The baby factory was so right. Who am I to pity her? She loves her job and wouldn't have it any other way. Maybe *my* personality and *my* choices make the job seem tough to *me*. The same way her personality and choices would have her writing her resignation letter with her own blood and tears within an hour of being tasked with *my* job. I no longer say anyone has a tougher job than anyone else because it's entirely subjective. Every woman is a unique and complex snowflake. And together we make up the mother of all storms.

I need my paycheck to pay for my retail therapy and to keep my freezer overflowing with meat and/or meat byproducts. But even if I didn't, I'm not sure I'd choose any differently. Maybe I'd work on my own terms. Write full time. Or invent a baby stroller that doubles as a hotdog stand. Or breed puppies. Or knit tea cozies (right after I learn how to knit and figure out what a tea cozy is). Or maybe I'd miss the excitement of the pitch, the creative collaboration of the big idea, and the water-cooler camaraderie of the working world. Maybe I would do what I'm doing now, by choice.

Truth is, as far as jobs go, I really like the one I have. It's fucking advertising! It's sex without the sperm all up in your grill! It's using words and pictures to communicate ideas, passionately selling them to clients, then seeing them out there in the real world compelling people to change their car, their hair, their habits. I won an award once for turning a banana peel into a trophy. "It's the cup final of composting," the headline read. A banana peel trophy, for excellence in composting. It was sexy as fuck. I just orgasmed.

The ad world sounds so exciting. But what I really do is read, listen to music, watch YouTube videos, troll the Internet, take a break to find out why Internet is capitalized, brainstorm with really smart people, bite my nails, stand on my head in my office, and inject tea directly into my veins—whatever it takes to conceive the next big idea by end of day Thursday. I'm just having a laugh, really. And they pay me for it. Okay, yes, it's super-fast paced and high-pressure, but I accept the chaos in exchange for the fun. As that 80s little girl who wondered why there was a Veterinarian Barbie but no Artist Barbie, this adsanity is a good fit for me. It's simple logic, really. My job makes me a happier, more complete person and that makes me a better mother. If I am happy, I teach Max happiness, right? Sure, the job keeps me away from him sometimes—when I'm on photo and TV shoots, or working long hours to meet crazy deadlines—but at least when I *am* with him, he gets the best of me. (If I'm stressed about a deadline and bring home that stress, I project it toward my husband. He's a big boy.)

I respect all mothers for their choice to work or stay at home, but I think it's important for each of us to be *more* than a mother. We are individuals with needs and talents and interests and opinions and fetishes. Or at least we were before we got impregnated. So for frig sake start talking about something besides how cute your kid's poop face is. Actually, the poop face is pretty darn cute, so keep talking about that. But most of the other stuff—mix it up a little, sister. Seriously. Don't lose the whole woman down the diaper pail.

Basket Case

Our house is about 900 square feet. Not a lot of space for a man, a woman, a dog, a kid, and a zillion big and little things that either entertain, clean, clothe, feed, or soothe said kid.

It wasn't so bad when Max was a cooing infant. I could organize the chaos around us, create a manger of inanimate onlookers with my swaddled miracle in his bouncy chair smack dab in the middle. There were breast pump attachments curled up on tabletops, receiving blankets and teeny tiny facecloths folded and stacked to the sky. It wasn't necessarily clean, but it was neat. Even the dirt was categorized into perfect little piles: cooties here, scuz there, crud up there, gook and gunk over there. Everything had its own spot or shelf or basket. There was even a basket for orphaned socks; as we all know, the dryer eats them.

"Another fuckin' basket?" the husband would scold when I'd bring home yet another wonder of wicker weavery.

He just didn't understand.

"It's not *just* a basket, honey. It's a cozy home for a bunch of crap. It's a *nest*!"

As my dad used to say, even Moses was a basket case.

Then, my perfectly immobile baby turned into a wrecking ball. I remember when I first declared on Facebook that he was walking. A co-worker and father of three boys commented, "Take it from me, push him down, push him down!" I quickly understood what he meant. Max skipped the walking stage and graduated right to demolition, his tootsies chauffeuring his hands to the next item on his list of "Things I Must Destroy." He climbed the couch, King Kong style, and threw the remote control behind it, where adult hands fear to forage. He hurled toys into the bathtub, then stood there watching them lie face down and helpless at the bottom of the porcelain ravine. He jabbed his mini hockey stick at the flat-screen

TV, a frequent cause of Daddy Angina. As soon as I put his wooden blocks into their designated basket, he dumped them out. And god forbid I try to build a tower with them. It came crashing down before it reached two blocks high, which means it was never actually a tower but a pathetic shack on a sticky floor.

Around his first birthday, sitting amidst the clutter, compounded by the dread of going back to work, I snapped! I needed to simplify this house and this life—pronto. A clutter-free home is a clutter-free mind, said Oprah. Amen, female black Jesus, amen. I realized the key to this endeavour was having less. Getting rid of the excess. Not necessarily spending less, but buying fewer—higher quality—things. Things that would withstand the test of time and the fury of Toddler Hitler.

So I started giving things to charity. And I started saying *no* to charity. Do I want your hand-me-downs? Nope. Stuff with stains on it? Get a grip. We're in Newfoundland, not Bangladesh. Unless you swallowed a twenty-four-karat gold nugget, I don't want your shit.

I was getting things under control, embracing my newfound simplicity. Then, just after his first birthday, I met someone, and my Almost Paradise began to unravel. His name? Thomas. The cheeky one. And he wasn't alone. He brought his whole red and green and brown and blue posse with him. There are trains and tracks everywhere: on the floor, in the couch, in my butt crack. Max goes to bed with a smiling locomotive in each hand and wakes up with them still in his death grip, often with a chassis impressed in his face. By his second Christmas, our living room had morphed into the Island of Sodor. If Sir Topham Hat walked through my front door right now, I would not be surprised. But *he* would get a startle, because he'd get a swift kick in those high-waisted pants for steaming over my dreams of minimalism.

And apparently this is just the beginning. Next up? Dinkies,[1] then Legos, then Transformers, then what? Little parts and doodads and gadgets up the yin yang. Clutter-free simplicity up in smoke. But hey, while my matchbox home is chock full of stuff and toys and

---

[1] You know, dinkies. Miniature toy cars. NOT the male genitalia, despite what *Urban Dictionary* suggests.

trains, my beautiful boy is brimming with joy. So what are ya gonna do? Buy more fuckin' baskets, that's what.

Silly Beaver

Perhaps I was a bee in a former life. Or maybe it was a beaver. Yeah, a beaver; beavers are really busy. I had buckteeth as a kid too. That settles it—I was once a beaver. There's a chewing on wood joke here somewhere, but I digress....

I complain about having too much to do, but truth is, I'm addicted to being busy. I need to be productive—creating something, building something, making something better. Now don't get me wrong. I don't need to be my mother's kind of busy—cleaning, cooking, and churning butter while knitting sweaters and cleaning the grout in the bathroom with a toothbrush. That's not my kind of busy.

I like to be on the move. Shopping: seeking the perfect sconce for that tiny bit of space between the toilet and the window. Writing: working on my dad's posthumous book of poetry and my own first work of heart which you now hold in your hands. Trying: new restaurants, new martini recipes, new trails, new sexual positions (not). I need to be constantly seeking something. A new vintage toy for my boy. The perfect metaphor. A great photo opp. A new idea. I wish I could just *be*. But alas, I am a beaver.

I know life is short; god, how short it is. So I remind myself daily to stop and smell the roses. Pet the dog. Cuddle the boy. Sip the tea. Maybe even choke the chicken. I'm good at being in the moment. I'm deep like that. I'm a writer for cryin' out loud; it's a curse. Sometimes I'm so in the moment, I forget to be in pants. But sometimes my high-speed nature gets the better of me. (Thanks for the loony genes, Mom.) Especially during holiday time with the hordes of people and endless traffic and lists of things to do propelling me to go go get 'er done NOW.

Holiday mall mopers? I hate them. And they travel in packs. So not only are they slow; they form an impenetrable wall of mope. I've daydreamed about making a fake bomb with an old car battery and some pipe cleaners, just to watch them scatter.

I start my Christmas shopping early so I don't have to stand in busy checkout lines when the holiday rush is on—a fate worse than death. Twenty percent off at the mall? No thanks. I'd rather pay twenty percent *more* to *not* stand in those lines. I hate waiting in line so much, I would consider deep-throating everyone ahead of me just to skip the queue.

A couple Christmases ago, the local Santa Claus parade started fifteen minutes late; I rained curses on the jolly old elf and his entire slow-ass entourage. It was cold and I had a little boy who kept flicking his mittens off. Time was of the essence. Digits were on the line. But I kept my patience, largely due to the friendly reminder I received earlier that day. A reminder to slow down, offered by an officer of the Royal Newfoundland Constabulary in the form of a speeding ticket. And yes, I am about to drop the f-bomb yet again. Fucking ghost car!

Despite my predicament, I was in a good mood, so I went with it. For a moment, I thought I would flutter my eyelashes a little and see if Goody Blue Shoes might be influenced by a fair damsel on her way to volunteer at the orphanage. Or to get her hair done, whatevs. But naw, that's not how I roll. So I decided to just own it. I screwed up, I admit. Now, how about a bit of tomfoolery to lighten the mood? I rolled down my window to greet him and said…

"Nice moustache!"

Okay, no I didn't. But I thought it. That crumb catcher was colossal.

What I actually said was, "Gosh darn it, officer, ya got me."

"License and registration, ma'am?"

I opened the glove compartment with glee. The kind of smile that hurts. "Pink sheet? Check. Blue sheet? Check. Got it, yay! Here ya go, officer."

"Do you know how fast you were going, Ms…Murphy?"

"Umm…one milllllllllion?"

"Ninety. In a sixty zone."

"Wow. My heavy foot disease must be acting up today."

Awkward laugh.

"Okay, wait here, Ms. Murphy."

He turned to walk back to his Decepticon.

"Hurry back!" I said with a genuine, Texas-size grin.

He came back with a yellow slip of paper.

"Yellow, my favourite colour. How did you know?"

I heard the faintest chuckle, muffled behind a curtain of upper-lip hair. His parting words: "Slow down, okay?"

"Oh I will. Slowing down is my favourite. Well, second favourite, after smiling."

I'm lucky he didn't give me the breathalyzer.

He did unknowingly give me some good advice though. And there's something I think we can all learn from my brush with the law: *slow down, bitches*. No matter how busy we are, let's not let it cloud our judgment. Let's not be so caught up in the little details that we forget to see the bigger picture. Of course we're gonna be beavers. It's in our nature. It's what we do. But let's do things a little more slowly, thoughtfully, and carefully. Not necessarily perfectly. Silly beave.

Boob-Tube Baby

"Moooo-veeee?"

This used to be Max's first word when he woke up in the morning. Now it's "iPad." Movies in your lap. Technology has come so far in his first few years of life.

Is this wrong? Maybe. Does it allow me to eat breakfast undisturbed? Hells to the yeah. So if my toddler being a movie junkie is wrong, then I don't wanna be right.

Okay, so I do wanna be right. I'm not Lindsay Lohan's mother for fuck's sake; I actually do want my kid to turn out normal. So I have to ask myself—is Max spending too much time with the electronic babysitter? Will too much boob tube make my boy a tit head?

There's this theory that too much video watching causes ADHD in small children. I hate to admit it, but it does make sense. A study by the American Academy of Pediatrics was published in 2004 proposing that

> the viewing of television by children less than two years of age is linked to the development of Attention Deficit Hyperactivity Disorder (ADHD) later in life…. How can we expect a child who is used to being entertained by flashing lights and quick moving animation to be interested in what their considerably less high-tech teacher is saying in front of the class?

I have just one thing to say in response to these scientific results: eek!

Maybe this explains Max's boggled facial expression when he watched *Cars*, or *Wall-E*, or *Toy Story 3* for the first time. He wasn't thinking, "Wow, cool, look at that!" He was thinking, "*What* the fuck is *that*?" Confusion escalated to terror when he saw *TS3*'s monkey with the cymbals. Can't blame him; that chimp makes me wanna go hide under the bed and suck my thumb.

I'd be sad to see *Toy Story 3* go; I've watched it about ninety-eight times and could watch it again right now and still be intrigued. Bless you, Disney Pixar. But part of me (my right hand, specifically) would be happy to take all the Thomas DVDs and put them in the blender. "They're two, they're four, they're six, they're…" *hate*! The theme song haunts my dreams. It's the soundtrack of our lives. What does shunting even mean? It sounds like the kind of sex you have when your parents are in town. "My folks are staying the night so we'll have to keep it down. We'll have to *shunt*."

Sometimes I also find myself spontaneously breaking into a British accent. This can't be healthy.

But that wretched song makes Max dance, so I gladly tolerate it. I know one day this stupid song and these little wooden trains will be treasures, placed on a high shelf somewhere—reminders of a simpler time when my little boy, now out there in the big world, was safely under my wing.

So…do I say, "No, Max, no more movies today"? Whining ensues, followed by the pouty face, then outright crying, then—my personal favourite—thrashing. When they pound their fists and foreheads on the couch—that's the best, isn't it? I know I need to ignore this behaviour so he knows it's not working, but that's easier said than done. His unjoy is a dog wrapped around my leg. I just want it to stop and after a long day at work I'll do anything to make it so—anything! And when one little flick of a play button can return us to complete and utter tranquility, how can I resist?

A friend of mine who heard about my TV addiction concerns offered me some reassurance. Count your blessings, she said. Her kid hates TV and begs for her attention 24/7. A stage-four clinger. That settles it. For the love of Lightning McQueen, press play.

Nonetheless, one day when Max had just turned two I decided to try something different. I called it Project Break-Free-From-TV. I gave the electronic babysitter the entire day off. (She's a bit of a square anyways.) And it was one of the best days ever. No movies. No Treehouse or Disney Channel. No computer. Daddy and Splash were off on a trek, so it was just us. Me and Max. And our imaginations.

First, we broke out the paper and crayons. He whined for a red ballpoint pen that was lying so irresistibly on the kitchen table. I gave in. He drew a fiery tornado and a ball of red yarn. We put it on the refrigerator. Like, on top of the fridge, not on the front. It wasn't *that* great.

Next, we read. He ripped the last remaining flaps out of a lift-the-flaps book. "Lift" or "rip." What's the diff? He was fully engaged in this book, and I was going with it, destruction and all.

Then we built a train track and played with the cheeky one and all his friends. I got down to his level, face to the floor, and pretended I was the voice of Percy (the green train) delivering the mail...or a deadly surprise! Ka-Boom!

Occasionally, I'd catch a glimpse of Max's face watching me. Total awe. Best feeling ever. I stayed down there for at least an hour. Damn, sometimes I wish we had carpet. My hemorrhoids would think carpet is just swell. Pun intended.

When I had exhausted my caboose, I opened the lid of the toy box where long forgotten gadgets were rediscovered. It was like the

Colony of Avalon[2] up in there. Max took his Fisher Price dog for a vigorous walk; thankfully the pooch hadn't wasted away after weeks of neglect. He picked up his Cabbage Patch Kid, stared into his lifeless eyes, and gave him a flick back into the abyss. Poor Dustin: one day, someone will comb your corn-silk hair and give you a second outfit, I promise.

For breakfast, he had a grapefruit and cereal—in a big boy *breakable* bowl. Shag it. Who cares if he breaks the bowl, as long as it's not on his eyeball, right?

At 10:30 a.m. we went to the gymnasium at the university, a Saturday morning ritual. He ran and jumped and swung as usual, and when it came time for the sing-a-long at the end, he actually sat down, clapped his hands, and did the actions to the songs with the other kids. What is this? *Focus?* A rarity for Mad Maximus Murphy.

For lunch, he ate fresh cod and nine Brussels sprouts. I sang as I cooked, extra jolly because I had just realized it's "Brussels," plural, with a capital B. Who knew? He swayed his hips and arms—his trademark move—to Mama's mediocre music. It was a peaceful meal. No television in the background. No leaning over the side of his highchair to see Handy Manny and his talking tools. It was just me and him and the sound of our chewing.

Next up—bath time. Sun poured in through the bathroom window as I leaned over to wash his copper curls. Everything was blissfully quiet, except for Max's laughter, the splashing of water, and the squeaky friction of his little butt cheeks on the bottom of the tub. While he played in the bubbles, I sat on the toilet and wrote a few thoughts down in my trusty notebook. Yes, the paper kind—imagine! As I was scribbling, a picture of my father fell out from between the pages and onto the floor. Well hello to you too, Poppy Jim; we're having a great day.

By 2:30 p.m. Max was zonked and ready for a nap. Break time for Mama, yeehaw. I had earned this, damn it. Hmmm, what would I do for the next 2.5 hours? Watch TV, of course! Psych. It crossed

---

[2] The Colony of Avalon is an archaeological site in Ferryland, on Newfoundland's Irish Loop, less than an hour from St. John's. The colony was founded in 1621 by George Calvert, aka Lord Baltimore. Hey losers in Baltimore, Maryland: we had him first.

my mind, but naw. I read a couple pages in a book—*A Short History of Nearly Everything* which is so not short at all—and caught forty winks on the couch.

At 5 p.m. I was awakened by a little voice down the hall. The second sweetest sound I could ever imagine, after "Vicki Murphy, come on down, you're the next contestant on *The Price is Right*."

We remained TV-free until bedtime, at which time we declared it was no longer 1876. Thirty minutes of a Thomas DVD and the little man was on the Sodor Express to dreamland.

Don't worry, we'll still be watching television. The next day, in fact, was Superbowl Sunday. Me and my "first-round draft pick" (he had a shirt that said that) planned to bust a move at half-time and watch for wardrobe malfunctions.

Seriously though, TV is great. In fact, I attribute at least a portion of my creative chops to *Mr. Dressup*. Ah, the crunch of those scissors through construction paper: it still makes me randy. And I credit a small but respectable fraction of my intelligence to Alex Trebek—that sexy, silver fox. Come on, don't lie. You know you've dreamed of sitting on that moustache too.

Single Parents: How in the Mother Do You Do It?

I am impatient by nature. Sometimes I stop pumping gas at the ten-dollar mark because standing there til the meter gets to fifty is pure, unadulterated torture. When I need to nuke something in the microwave for a minute, I press 1:11, because pressing 1:00 would take a hundred years with those zeroes way the fuck down there at the bottom of the keypad. Sometimes I even cut off my pee before my bladder is fully emptied.

Max has been the biggest indicator of this and many other character flaws of mine. When he's a teenager, I'm sure he will readily point out even more. While carving "Mom is a Bitch" inside his closet with a pocketknife.

So this is written by that tragically imperfect part of me, but most of it is inspired by pure curiosity: how do single parents do it? Those solo flyers who, regardless of how impatient or frustrated or overwhelmed they are, have no second-in-command to take the helm. No one to relieve them for a moment, let alone an hour or a day. I am mystified by this. Discombobulated. Flummoxed. And other big words that help emphasize my wonder. How the frig do you people do it without dunking someone's head in a pot of boiling water every hour?

I have just one toddler and, luckily, a very competent partner. But, on occasion, it's just me and Max—at the doctor, or the swimming pool, or the mall, or a restaurant. And while at the end of the day it feels good to have spent this precious one-on-one time together, when it's happening it's a little bit of a total bloody nightmare.

Case in point: our trip to the ophthalmologist when Max was two. Daddy was working, so Maximus and Mama went as a duo. Dynamic? Not so much. But I thought, "It's a simple eye appointment. How bad could it be?" The answer: pretty fuckin' bad. I mean first of all, this was going to entail poking at his eyes. Not his arms or his legs or his ears. His *eyes*. The part of him that *sees* what you are trying to do to him. I can't even deal with that puff of air blown into my eye at the optometrist once a year (because it's downright terrifying), how could I expect Max to allow some white-coated stranger to poke and prod and squirt a foreign substance into his baby browns? Exactly. I can't blame the little guy for his behaviour. But that doesn't mean I didn't want to strangle him with the drawstring in his stupid little jogging pants.

First of all, let me rewind twenty-five minutes. Just in case the hospital parking situation was the usual calamity, we showed up a little early for our appointment. You'd think this would be a good thing, right? Think again, foolio. The lesson of the day: never show up early for anything with a person under three-feet tall. Unless he's a funny and candy-filled imp. First of all, the clinic is never going to be on schedule. I don't know why they even bother giving appointment times. They should just tell you to come on down and hang out for a couple of hours. And the longer you're there waiting, of course, the more damage your child will do to the waiting room and that part of you that makes you not a serial killer.

I had cleverly brought Max's stroller—a child-size straightjacket on wheels. But once I let him out of the damn thing, it morphed into a steamroller. Max had turned on the Turbo Ginger, rolling over people's feet with the stroller, bumping into other strollers, and slamming it into the fish tank while shouting, "Crash!" I would have taken the thing away, but there was nowhere to put it except in the ever-widening furl of my brow. I tried to distract him with juice, with raisins, with my iPhone, but even the most kickass *Thomas the Tank Engine* app could not charm him. A too-relaxed-looking father nearby casually remarked that I had my hands full, then proceeded to advise me.

"I just let them go," he said. "Just let them do their thing. Everybody understands."

Oh really? So everyone just smiles with understanding when my kid *crashes* into their shins? Is that why that woman over there just gave me the hairy eyeball? Because she *understands*? Is that couple over there cool with my sticky-fingered son poking their newborn baby in the retina? The mother of the little girl who was touching the train sticker on the wall whose arm Max was swiping at angrily because that sticker was "mine!" She enjoys seeing her kid mauled, does she? Yeah, okay buddy. Thanks for the tip. I'd love to get your soon-to-be-ex-wife's take on your easy-going philosophy.

Finally we hear the magic words: "Max Murphy." Thank you, sweet saviour. I grabbed the stroller and proceeded to pry his fingers from the handles. Ouch—he bit my hand! I ripped his fingers free and, out of pure spite, he took a bite out of the foam handle of the stroller. Little idiot. I scooped the black chunk out of his mouth with one swift swoop of my finger, grabbed up all our stuff—stroller, coats, purse, diaper bag, pile of rubble—and dragged the mini demon by the arm toward the doc's office. He fought me every step of the way, his head thrown backward toward the ceiling, his back arched toward the floor. Son of a me.

Before we saw the doctor, the nurse had to put some "preliminary drops" in Max's eyes. Oh great, so we gotta endure this *twice*? We pinned him down and forced his eyelids open. Mission accomplished (so far). Then we had twenty minutes before we saw the doctor. So I did the only logical thing. I beelined to the cafeteria and bought a bag of two-bite brownies. Maybe if he was chowing down on some sugary sweet chocolate, he wouldn't notice us prying open his eyeballs and squirting liquid in there for a second time? It was worth a shot.

As expected, the appointment with the ophthalmologist was intense. My boy's no dummy; he learned from the first encounter in this office and had since evolved into a superior being. He immediately tried to escape the room. I had to stand in front of the door because some genius had installed those flip-handle doorknobs that even a fetus could open. And since we're talking design flaws, the floor—could it get any harder? Great for cracking the skulls of thrashing toddlers. Might as well have chairs made of plutonium and sledgehammer-machete chandeliers dangling from the ceiling. One sec, I gotta run to the vending machine for a bag of glass shards.

When I laid eyes on the doctor, I was like "uh maaaan." She was a Lilliputian, for Swift's sake! I was hoping for a hulk-like creature who could pin Max down with his pinky finger and get this thing done and over with. The good doctor and I used every ounce of our combined strength to get the fluorescent orange drops into Max's eyes. I pinned his feet between my legs and held his arms with my hands while she tried to steady his big ol' flailing melon. Turbo Ginger would not relent.

I asked the doctor if this behaviour was normal. She replied, "Yes, we get about one a day." Well then, considering she sees fifty to sixty kids every day, that's comforting. My kid's a freak.

When the worst was over, she tried to explain Max's tear-duct problem to me with the use of a lovely diagram. But it's a little hard to focus on the science when the subject is wigging out, still reeling from this third-world torture. I took a mental snapshot of the moment: Max, two eyes trimmed with bright orange like he had lost a fight with a pumpkin, gripping a brownie so tightly it's crumbling all over the floor, flashing chocolate-covered teeth, and sobbing angrily while swiping at zillion-dollar gadgets on the doctor's desk. What a beaute. I pulled him away from trouble with every third word out of the doctor's mouth. She may as well have been telling me "The brown fox jumped over the white fence." I nodded and thanked her and got the hell outta Dodge.

As I wheeled my tiny terror away (oh yes, he was in that stroller and staying there until we reached the far end of the parking lot), a couple things hit me:

1. My decision to not have another child right now. Yup, good call, Self. If I had a second child with me just now, someone would be going up for adoption.

2. And how the hell do single parents do it? Kudos, also, to those whose spouses work away from home half their lives, and those who are raising families far away from the helping hands of other family members—that much-needed relief from time to time. Wow. Parenthood is a tough job at the best of times. I can't imagine doing it all alone. Without someone to take over while I recharge the batteries in my patience machine.

So to all you solo acts out there, I say this with the utmost respect and admiration: I salute you. I see ya. But I wouldn't wanna be ya.

Romance: Gone the Way of the Placenta

Valentine's Day…meh.

It takes me about a week to shake off the sugar coma. But hey, works for me. Some people are more creative on marijuana; my drug of choice is the choc. (Some people utilize both of nature's gifts, hence "special brownies," which I have never tried, by the way, except maybe twice.) It's the glucose working its brain-boosting magic. But it's short-lived, of course. The sugar rush wears off and I return to my dark place, which I wish was made of cocoa, but nope—it's just darkness.

V-Day. Who came up with this day that, abbreviated, sounds more like a disease you contracted in college? Hallshey, that's who. (Hallmark + Hershey = the Valentine's Day conspiracy.) Seriously, it's an excuse to fatten our asses and the wallets of those freakin' magicians at Lindt. It's a time to buy insanely overpriced greeting cards, 90% of which say what you could have easily said yourself for zero dollars and eighteen seconds of actual self-induced thought. Why not put five bucks in an envelope with a handwritten note that says, "I almost spent this five dollars on a stupid card but I thought it'd be better off in your pocket next to your cute little crotch." There ya go. Next year's card for your spouse. Done. You're welcome. Valentine's Day is rationale to buy new earrings and pretend your husband bought them even though he secretly thinks you're a total imbecile for buying yet another frivolous item that could have paid for six months of the NHL network and twelve wobbly pops to boot.

Or maybe this is just the voice of a woman whose husband is not exactly the romantic type anymore. Sure, he has his moments, but beyond the occasional loving squeeze, chivalry is dead. Okay, it's on life support. And no, honey, slapping my ass or waving your dick around like a tassle on a showgirl's tit does not constitute romance. How about I slap your ass while you're washing the dishes, polishing your Vicki shrine, and desperately seeking a medical breakthrough that enables men to give birth?

Men! Why do they stop complimenting us? Like most husbands, Andrew would counter this question with another question: "Why do women stop swallowing our sperm?" Well played, husband, well played.

But get a clue, sucka foo. After all these years, do you still not realize that flattery and fornication are attached at the hip? You are all so dumb. So very, very dumb.

Moments before I completed this womanuscript, I told my husband I would dedicate my book to him, to thank him for all his support. I was trying to start something sweet. You know, throw a compliment his way, see if I might get one back, followed by some cuddling and possible afternoon delight. His response? "That book wouldn't exist without me anyway, because I am the one who got you pregnant with my meat cannon."

I remember a few years back, after a significant PDA[3] dry spell, I overheard Andrew tell his friend that I was beautiful. He

---

[3] Public Displays of Affection

MotherFumbler

was a little drunk, talking a little too loudly, and had no idea I had heard. I mean, god forbid I hear it! My head might triple in size and I'd leave him for another man who, ironically, showers me with compliments (in spite of my now oversized head).

Now, during times when I'm looking particularly good with no validation from the hubby, I think back to that "beautiful" remark. That one word, overheard all those years ago, has kept me from driving my fingers into his brain via his nostrils. Kind words have great longevity. And that word was particularly potent because it was spoken in secret, so I knew he meant it.

But alas, I share the blame. I am not the same spontaneous tart I once was. Responsibility has sucked the fun out of me. If only stress was a turn-on; that'd be deadly:

"Honey, the property tax is due. $1,100. Woot. Whip out the checkbook—and those sexy satin pajamas I like. You're gonna dip your pen in my inkwell."

"Babe, Max is crying again. I just adore the sound of his frantic wailing, don't you? Let's make out."

"I gotta work again this weekend, honey. Bow chicka wow wow. I get so randy when I'm overworked. It's like the exhaustion makes me want to love you long time."

I may not be quite the free spirit I once was, but hey, I'll always be crazy. Crazy is fun, right? Right?

Relationships change and evolve. It's just the way the nookie cookie crumbles. People change and evolve. And so we should. This is why it's wise to wait to get married until you're thirty, maybe more. We are constantly growing and changing, especially during our twenties when we don't even know who we are because we spend all our time wondering who other people think we are, and trying to be that. We are a cocktail of hormones and self-doubt. There ya go, twenty-somethings; serve that at your nuptials.

Unfortunately, our biological and emotional clocks are not in sync. The female body is primed for pregoville at age fifteen. Precisely the age when the female brain is at its dumbest. So sometimes our bodies thrust us toward marriage and motherhood before the clay in our heads has even begun to dry. Our bodies are all juiced up and ready for action. Our minds are on a carousel, constantly twirling and swirling with uncertainty and "Cha-cha-cha-changes."

We are still changing now, in our thirties and forties and fifties. We're always changing because we're always learning.

I took the plunge at age thirty. If I had waited to get hitched, would I have chosen someone different? Probably. It's no offense to Andrew; it's just simple fact. The older version of myself would have been looking for a partner through a different set of eyes. Maybe wiser eyes. Maybe darker, more skeptical eyes. But different eyes.

But alas, I think there is an essence, a core in each of us that stays wholly the same. Maybe we are OH Henry! bars. The nuts and caramel swirl around, ever changing as we get older, but the nougat at the centre holding it all together stays the same. So as we learn and evolve and doubt and question everything, we remember the nougat. It's about more than nuts.

Instead of giving in to doubt and jumping ship, we love the one we're with and support one another through the constant evolution of life. You know, as long as he's not constantly beating the life out of you. Lord knows it's not easy; a good, honest, reliable, kind, and entertaining copilot is a necessity and a blessing if you should be lucky enough to find such a creature who's not of the canine variety. Through thick and thin, boredom and challenge, sickness and health, sugar rushes and sleep deprivation, we keep the love alive in all its glorious imperfection.

So I dedicate this chapter to my man-thing. Here are a few verses from a poem I wrote and recited at our wedding. Yes, I really did. His ninety-four-year-old grandmother especially loved the part where I called him a human erection.

REASONS
For being happy to see me after a short time apart.
For sharing things with me, like your dreams
    and your farts.
For calling me at 4 a.m. in an inebriated state.

For boldly trying to tongue me on our first freakin'
date.

For embracing my weirdness instead of running for
the hills.

For being right smart with your scientific skills.

For your great sense of humour and getting all
my jokes.

For knowing the Heimlich maneuver. You know,
in case I choke.

For never taking for granted the woman that
you've got.

Or the lunatic I tend to be more often than not.

For being a man of outward affection. (Not really.)

For being tall and trim, like a human erection.

For your scruffy unshaven face that gives my thighs
a rash.

For supporting me with your spirit instead of mere
cash. (Get a job.)

For being a loyal friend. For loving our dog.

For being a big fat remote control hog.

For hanging the tree lights with anal perfection.

For sharing with me your wicked beer bottle
collection.

For appreciating the sarcasm of the previous line.

For being the perfect other half in this two-of-a-kind.

For giving me things that simply can't be bought.

These are the reasons I love you.

Hey, how could I not?

Dear Husband, Are You Fucking Blind?

The hubby got off easy in the last story. Enough of that.

I'm a mommy blogger. Naturally, my main subject is my
main man, Max Murphy. But marriage is so intimately tied to

motherhood—if you manage to survive the turbulent toddler years without killing each other—that my husband often creeps up in my writing. Not unlike the way he crept up into my bootyliciousness some nine years ago at a club downtown.

In spite of inevitable marital disputes, I try to respectfully hold back on the husband bashing. Hence, there is no chapter in this book called "My Husband Is a Jackass." But not for lack of material.

Still, I reckon after two consecutive long weekends of fishing, golfing, and drinking, followed by a night out with his friends that delivered his hairy ass home at 4:30 a.m. reeking of George Street sausage dogs and whores—he's fair game.

See, some husbands must endure the wrath of the wife who nags, yells, throws things, and generally freaks her freak. And some husbands are subject to the wife who gently types. La la la, I'm typing, I love to type, typing is my life. He needn't know that with every key softly pecked I'm stabbing someone with a rusty butter knife and a smile.

Not that he even reads anything I write. He probably just scans for the words "husband" and "Andrew." Maybe he should also start scanning for "douchebag" and "tit head," starting right now.

See, I found some photos on his camera. Photos of him and his fishing buddies spooning in a tent, lovingly feeding each other beans from a can, and getting jiggy under the light of the moon.

Just kidding.

It was actually much, much worse. Brace yourself. The photos were…NOT. OF. ME. Gasp!

I mean obviously he didn't take any photos of me on his fishing trip. Because I was not there on the bloody fishing trip. I have bigger fish to fry, thank you very much. My point is—he never takes pictures of me. Ever. Not pictures of me. Not pictures of me and Max together. According to the camera roll on his iPhone, we don't exist. Not even the George Street strumpets get to see how cute we are.

I mean, god forbid he acknowledge my classic ginger beauty with an art form that does not include slapping my ass and yelling "giddy-up!"

Maybe if I had three months to live he might consider immortalizing my image with a camera. I mean maybe. Possibly. If he didn't have anything better to do. As long as it's not fishing season.

But it's not that he doesn't take *any* photos. Oh, he takes photos. Of fish. And fish next to beer bottles to show how big (and photogenic) said fish are. Now that's something special.

I'm always the one behind the lens. What? Producing an heir wasn't enough? Now I am also the sole photo-biographer of our lives? There are so many snapshots of Andrew and Max, I was able to make an epic slideshow for him for Father's Day.

Number of pics of *me* and Max? Four. And all four of them were taken during Max's first few minutes of life, when I finally held him on the *outside*. He was perfect; rocked a blue flannel blanket like it was nobody's business. I looked like a manatee washed up on the beach after a three-hour rumble with a shark. A sea cow in a paisley johnny shirt. Oh yeah baby. Get at me. There's nothing sexier than a cow right after she calves. Let's go upload these smokin' snaps to my Facebook and watch as messages from would-be suitors flood in like afterbirth into a bowl. I'll be sure to block the entire state of Florida; they might send wildlife authorities to bring me back.

I'm surprised I wasn't the one taking the pictures. Birthing-suite selfies—newborn in one arm, Nikon in the other, knob in an armchair across the room sucking a popsicle.

I'm being a dramatic slop-tart. Obviously, Andrew has taken more than four photos of me in our time together.

He has taken five.

And here's the kicker—I had to *ask* him to take all five. There are few things in life I love more than begging someone to take my picture. I mean, it just makes me feel so humble and modest and not at all obsessed with my own face. He sighs, giving in. Now that's a sound that really makes a girl feel beautiful. Just let me take my clothes off right now. And my smile as he carelessly snaps the picture—it just doesn't get any more genuine. Look at the sparkle in my eye....

That's not a sparkle, honey. That's a volt of electric rage. I made you a fucking SLIDESHOW!

After he takes the shot, he hands the camera back or pockets the phone immediately. That's it, one shot. No need to see how the ol' heffer turned out. I could have had my eyes closed, my tit hanging out, anything. It doesn't matter. He exerted so much energy, depleted every ounce of creative juice with this one act of photographic genius, he couldn't possibly take one more for good luck.

And just to clarify, so all you bushpigs out there don't come at me with comments like "get over yourself," I'm not asking him to take my picture because I think I'm hot as balls. I'm asking him to take it so that, in the event of my untimely death, Max will know I bloody well existed! Is that so much to ask? How much do you remember from age three? Exactly. If I die tomorrow, all Max will have to remember me by are these silly stories, a handful of crappy photos, and a belly button.

But I'm not going to give up on my other main man just yet. Next time our little family finds itself someplace magical, with the salty Atlantic breeze tossing our ginger manes to and fro, the setting sun casting the perfect golden light on our freckled faces, I will give him the opportunity to make his move. I will give him the chance— about forty-five seconds—to stop taking pictures of his balls and emailing them to his friends, and start taking pictures of something bigger. Something beautiful that, sadly, just won't last.

Enough with the tadpoles, honey. It's time to take a picture of *all a dis*. The catch of your fuckin' life.

Douchebag.

Tit head.

In fairy tales, it's always the children
who have the fine adventures.
The mothers have to stay at home and wait
for the children to fly in the window.

— AUDREY NIFFENEGGER, *THE TIME TRAVELER'S WIFE*

CHAPTER FOUR

Playing Mommy

Life as I know it is over. But another life has sprung from the scar tissue. And it's a life that feels oddly familiar. Because in some ways (with extra emphasis on "some"), it's the life I used to have.

Despite becoming a mother, an adult responsible for the well-being of a child, I have never felt like such a kid. I am rediscovering the wonders of the world with my wide-eyed wonder boy. Honey, I shrunk the mommy! I had completely forgotten how the world looks from way down here. How very big things are! Holy shit, Max, look at the hams on Nanny! And look at the dust bunnies living under the couch! Die, bunnies, die!

Some of my earliest memories are of toys. Ask me about being seven and one of the first things that comes to mind is my Speak & Spell. Ask me about being nine and there's this toy called the Fuzzy Farm—a green velvet board with a bunch of velvety barnyard animals that I arranged on the surface to create a farm scene. I don't remember where I was playing or with whom, but I remember the object. The toy carries the memory for me. How it smelled. How it felt. And how it made me feel.

Sometimes I find myself just watching Max, his eyes twinkling with WTF. Captivated by a worm in the driveway or popcorn kernels popping or a crackling campfire. I remember the first time Max saw a bubble. Total fascination. And you know, it got me thinking: what the heck *are* bubbles anyway? Perfect spheres created by some soapy water. What the...? How is this possible? But wait, there's more. When two bubbles meet, the smaller one bulges into the bigger one. And if a whole bunch of bubbles meet, they form hexagons. Like, what? Come again. My head just exploded. Bubbles: a seventy-nine-cent bottle of blow-your-fuckin'-mind.

The world I've grown weary of is pretty cool after all. I am a child again. Max is my very own fountain of youth. So...why do I look so haggard?

Working for the Geekend

Ah yes, May 24th weekend turned geekend. Ten years ago, I was probably cracking open a six-pack on some crappy campground in rubber boots, a tube top, and a scrunchie. Now, I sit at home cracking open a six-pack...of delectable Maple Leaf Vienna sausages.

The kids change things a tad, no? "Partying" now entails cake, sticky fingers, loot bags that should include a coupon for a free root canal, and shit on the wind. Okay whose kid got the job done?

But I'll have you know, I don't stay home during the nation's unofficial outdoor party of the year because it's the motherly thing to do. I stay home because the weather on Victoria Day weekend here in Newfoundland is, ironically, a lot like Queen Victoria's royal chuff-box—soggy and miserable.[1] A funky cold vagina. And we don't have a forty-foot camper. And as lovely as the gravel pit[2] sounds, I think I'll put on my jammies, curl up on the couch, watch cartoons with my boy, and pretend these sausages are not made of lips and

[1] Actually, while Queen Victoria was known as the ultimate prude (her famous quote: "We are not amused.") it is rumoured she was quite amused by the ol' dude piston and frequently went bumpin' nasties in the royal boudoir.

[2] In Newfoundland, camping in unused gravel pits is a common summer pastime. All class, baby. (Google "The Pits" by Buddy Wassisname and the Other Fellers.)

assholes. Besides, if I was wearing a tube top right now, it'd be hanging somewhere between my ribs and my hips. And that, happy campers, just ain't right.

Has motherhood sucked the fun out of me? No doubt it has tamed and softened me a little. I cried watching Mary Hart's farewell episode on *Entertainment Tonight* a couple years back. That shit was emotional. And let's face it, I work hard fifty-plus hours a week with socialization and collaboration up the wazoo; call me a stick in the mud, but sometimes I just need to do nudding with nobody. But I still have a wild side, damn it. Take these toxic sausages for instance. Six little cylindrical logs of rebel yell.

For me, motherhood is about balance. A place somewhere between giving it all you got and giving zero fucks. I buy whole-grain Cheerios, for example. *But*, I put spilled Cheerios back in the box. In my house, the five-second rule is not only enforced, it's encouraged. We actually rub things on the floor for five seconds before we put it on the plate. Spaghetti night at our house is like a murder scene.

I curse. A lot. I'm in advertising, so it's either swearing or smoking, and last I checked f-bombs don't kill you; they just sound like they might. But I am tailoring my diction to include apt substitutes like "Shoot," "Cheez Whiz," "Gosh darn it," "Fick," "Feck," "Fack," and "Fudge." It feels like my tongue is in a straightjacket, but at least it's not in a giant toilet.

I share ridiculous, self-deprecating things on social media, like "I am now going for a jog, with my ass in a sidecar driving alongside." And, "Prize: baby. Parting gifts: hemorrhoids." And, "Jam out with your clam out!" How unladylike. How unmotherly. Oh bite it. I type to entertain. At least I'm not a sixteen-year-old girl with an iPhone glued to my face and a thong halfway up my back—the future of our world, by the way. We are all, like, totally screwed.

I let Max watch *Dexter*. When there's a horrendous crime scene, I point to the window and say "Look, Max, a birdie!" He hardly even notices the blood-curdling screams in the background. I have a master's degree in the art of distraction.

It's all okay. This badass mommy goes to therapy. At the mall. I usually don't buy much because the vast majority of things are made by somebody's blind great-great grandpa in Beijing. Most times I just walk around, smile at pretty things, hold them, and then put them back. It helps.

I don't party often, but when I do, I make a concerted effort to have fun. And I don't see anything wrong with dressing sexy. One day, when I am as saggy as a pillowcase full of meat, I will wish I had worked this ass a little more. But I don't dress skunty; there's a difference. And occasionally, I ride big giant inflated penises on party buses. (Insert pic here? Naw.) After which time my mother calls and instructs me to delete the photo from my Facebook. Don't be tagging me in your photos, people. Unless the setting is a church or a seniors' home or a country meadow. Scratch the country meadow, actually. Damn you, spring break '98.

I like to dance, but I don't grind strange men downtown. In fact, I try not to make skin-on-skin contact with any human within a 500-yard radius of George Street. I just kinda party in my own little martini bubble then roll it toward a cab like a hamster in a ball.

I stay out late, but not too late because I have a toddler who's going to wake me up with a plastic chainsaw or power drill in a handful of hours. And honestly, I want to enjoy that day with him, not be hungover like a rack of tits. Every day has immense value in this pathetically brief life.

And I always come home to my husband because, well, that's where I want to be at the end of the day. Not because it's my duty; because it's my preference. And there's no place cozier than the thickets of his back hair.

Some people constantly talk about the days of yore. Former loves. Badass parties. Longing for that time when they were young, wild, and free. I get a little nostalgic sometimes, especially when I hear any song from *Dance Mix* '90 to '95. But those memories usually conclude with "Man, I really dodged a bullet there."

I don't yearn for the past, but if I did, it'd have nothing to do with partying downtown or long weekends camping. I would ache for the days long before that, when I'd put my hands straight by my sides and make fists and Dad would lift me up into the air "to see if you're a Newfie." And I'd long for the recent past, when my son was a baby pointing his chubby finger at everything in his big, shiny new world. "Wha da?" he'd softly say, over and over again. Andrew and I watch home videos with tears welling up behind our smiles, mourning for a time we'll never see again, knowing this is a feeling we'll have to get used to.

I don't miss my single life one little bit. I miss childhood. Mine. And the one that's happening so quickly right before my eyes.

Growing Up. Boo

Halloween ain't what it used to be. (Neither is Christmas. Or Easter. Or even Fridays.) But it's not the tradition that has changed. It's me.

When I was a child, Halloween was full of a spooky kind of magic. The night sky was always black with streetlights beaming certainty in scattered parts of our quaint seaside town. I grazed from house to house, floral pillowcase in hand, brimming with excitement. Mom would hide around the corner while Raggedy Ann or Strawberry Shortcake or Little Orphan Annie (all obvious costume choices) knocked on each door and delivered the trio of magic words—Trick or Treat? Once my load was heavy with sugar, it was time to head home to dump my cargo into a heap on the living-room floor. Now, to blissfully sort. Candy here. Chocolate there. Chips and cheezies over there. And a handful of rare treasures: a small pack of crayons, a pencil, a teeny tiny notebook. What a haul.

Somewhere between childhood and womanhood, between hockey hair and marvelous mane, Halloween, among other things, lost its luster. Maybe ghouls and goblins suddenly seemed ridiculous now that I knew the jolly old elf was a hoax and a half. "Where there is no imagination, there is no horror," said Sir Arthur Conan Doyle. Maybe I discovered what OD-ing on junk food does to the teeth and the tushie. I don't remember exactly when things changed or why, but they did. I guess with age comes wisdom, and wisdom comes at the price of wonder.

Don't get me wrong. I've had my adult fun with Halloween. Around age twenty, I realized Halloween afforded me the rare, judgment-free opportunity to dress like a total slut. So I seized the day. But hey, at least I was creative! There are far too many slutty cops, slutty nurses, and slutty schoolgirls running around out there. How unoriginal are twenty-year-old girls anyway? If you're going to dress like a bimbo, at least be clever about it. Be a slutty nun, a slutty sous chef, or a slutty beekeeper. A few years ago, myself and Andrew dressed up as Little Miss Muffet (the naughty version) and the spider (you know, the one who sat down beside her). My arachnid hubby sported an extra "leg," and his shirt said, "What's in the bowl, bitch?" On the back of my dress was written, "Sit on my tuffet." Whey too much fun.

Maybe motherhood has indeed softened me. Or maybe I've just evolved into a different, more self-preserving kind of party girl. No mistake, I live for the absurd. And I can finish off a bottle of red wine before the cork stops rolling. But the parameters of my merrymaking are different now. Take last Halloween, for example. In bygone years, I would have attended Mardi Gras on George Street[3] —my old stomping grounds of singlehood. But nope, not interested. I took my tiny terror to a kid's Halloween party instead. I went as primetime's fave fangbanger, Sookie Stackhouse. Andrew was Vampire Bill (if you don't know these characters, it's because you don't watch *True Blood* and we can't be friends). Max was decked out as—again, working with the ginger as my mother taught me— Satan! That night, instead of rocking the streets of downtown, I rocked Beelzebub Boy to sleep. I chose to eat candy, cuddle with the fur kid, watch *Poltergeist*, and just breathe. If that makes me a crusty old lady, you can kiss my crusty ass.

I miss the Halloweens of childhood. But the spirit of it all is not entirely lost on me; it is rekindled through my Max. During his second Halloween at age eighteen months, I savoured his mystified look as neighbours plopped treats into his pumpkin. He was too young to understand, but every twinkle in his eye counted for something, molding him into a person-shaped chunk of happiness. At

---

[3] George Street is a small, cobblestone street in St. John's, Newfoundland, with the most bars and pubs per square foot of any street in North America. According to a *MacLean's* magazine survey, St. John's has the sexiest people in the world. You'll find some of them on George Street. Just lift their heads off the bar and look at their sexy faces.

Christmas, I saw that twinkle when he feasted his eyes on the multi-coloured lights, his new wooden train track under the tree, and when he came face to face with Mr. Kringle himself (the most wonderful lie of all time).

I also hope that Max, one day, mourns his childhood as I do. Because that will mean I didn't screw him up too bad after all.

> The greatest poem ever known
> Is one all poets have outgrown:
> The poetry, innate, untold,
> Of being only four years old.
>
> —CHRISTOPHER MORLEY, "TO A CHILD"

A Toy Story

The toy people are pretty sneaky. Bringing back all the toys from the 80s to play on the sentiment of the thirtyish crowd who are now parents with Christmas lists longer than Barbie's luxury limo. Every toy section is a labyrinth of dolls and trucks and games and gadgets. A multi-billion-dollar industry indeed. What's going to catch *my* attention? The familiar face of a Cabbage Patch Kid smiling back at me, of course. (RIP, Casey Gwendolyn.)

Or a Smurf. "La la la la la la…la la la la la." Best lyrics ever.

My Little Pony. I brushed that horse's hair til the cows came home.

The Etch-a-Sketch. A love child of the 60s, it's the great-great-grand-daddy of Photoshop. And it's so simple to use. I mean, why draw with crayons on paper when you can twist knobs to move a stylus to displace aluminum powder on the back of a screen in a plastic frame?

Strawberry Shortcake. I had the complete bedding set: bedspread, curtains, pillow shams, booyah. I can still smell her. (That's what he said.)

These 80s fads and more are all back with a GI Joe-caliber vengeance. I'm holding out for a Popple—the "soft fuzzy ball that turns into a friend." Who needs a friend *with* soft fuzzy balls when you can have a friend who *is* a soft fuzzy ball?

The other day, I saw a Monchiichi and for a moment I was six years old again, minus the buckteeth and achy-breaky haircut.

Every jar of Play-Doh slingshots me back to a time and a place when life was as simple as a Rubiks Cube. Er…scratch that. A Slinky. That's better. It was a time when fun was all that mattered. When my problems extended no further than my Flintstones toy box.

Max is just a toddler, so most of these retro toys are too advanced for him. He'd bake *himself* in the EasyBake Oven. Gingerbread, anyone? But he does have a couple of truly classic toys in his stash, in all their uncomplicated, no-instruction-booklet-no-assembly-or-batteries-required glory.

1. The jack-in-the-box. This toy dates back to the Middle Ages, invented by some dude named Jack who got in a box and popped out and everybody laughed. Max has a Sock Monkey jack-in-the-box. Crank the lever to churn out the classic yet creepy "Pop Goes the Weasel" and—BOING!—a Sock Monkey, doing a poor job at pretending to be a weasel, springs out from inside. But baby Max was frightened shitless of the thing. As soon as I started to turn the handle, he'd back up in sheer terror. And when the song came to an end and the monkey popped up, his lips would wriggle with dread, a prelude to tears. And yet, seconds later, he'd set the little metal box on my lap. "Do it again, Mommy," his big brown eyes beseeched me. Early signs of a sadomasochist? Just a little boy with balls, I hope.

2. Wooden blocks. These date back a trillion years. I bet young Jesus had such blocks; his father was a carpenter for Christ's sake (SFX: short drum roll with cymbal crash). Max's blocks are extra classy, each one sporting the Montreal Canadiens' logo. A gift from Daddy, straight from the Bell Centre. They're chunkier than most blocks you'll find in stores, a better fit for a curious but clumsy hand. Though they feature letters, numbers, and pictures to boot, Max has learned nothing from them except how to incorporate them into his arsenal of weapons. Pine is the softest wood, thankfully.

3. The spin top. This toy is older than dirt. In fact, clay tops were uncovered in the ancient city of Ur, near modern-day Baghdad, dating back to 3500 BC. Even Shakespeare wrote about the "whipped top" in his play *The Merry Wives of Windsor*. To us, it's a classic toy from the 1960s, revived in the 1990s, and still adding a touch of old school charm to playrooms everywhere.

Motherhood has rekindled my love of toys and gives me a great excuse to play with them. I admit, I gave Max a Cabbage Patch Doll so I could smell those powder-fresh buttocks.

Wait til you see my Lego wine rack.

Classic Toys for Poor Kids

Are we still in a recession? Not sure what the official word is from the money people. But let's face it, unless you're striking oil or gold or the next big idea in the Harry Potter franchise (because you're JK Rowling), you is po'. How in god's name does anyone afford to buy a home these days? I see these ginormous houses being built and I'm like "What do those people do?" It's got to be drug money. They definitely don't have kids. Or maybe the kids are running the meth lab. Nice cover.

Kids are expensive. But my lack of a social life cushions the cost, so it kind of works itself out. But I do have to be cautious of overspending in the face of so many cute outfits and baby gadgets and—dare I say it again—toys!

How many of you have given your kid a gift only to watch him or her toss the pricey present aside and play with the damn wrapping paper? And when your poor deprived offspring have opened their skyward heap of gifts, don't they often pick the cheapest thing to play with first? Why waste your hard-earned money? Max is getting one gift for Christmas this year—a telescope. And by telescope, I mean an empty paper towel roll.

Here are a few classic, and I mean *really* classic, toys for your wee ones. Each one fosters imagination and creativity, and guess what? They're all *free*!

1. The Cardboard Box. A classic among children everywhere. It comes with a built-in, saloon-style door, and windows can be installed custom. (Well, more like cut-out than put-in. Even easier.) The cardboard box is incredibly multi-functional. It can be a house, a cave, a hospital, or a totally pimped out go-cart. For entrepreneurial kids, it makes a kickass lemonade stand. People spend a fortune on these child-size kitchens, but why? Just toss a few pots and pans in the box and your pint-size chef is good to go, money saved. For easy storage, the cardboard box can be folded flat and stored under the couch or bed. Sizes may vary. A refrigerator box equals a swagadelic luxury hotel.

2. The Blunt Stick. Please note: this is different from the Sharp Stick, which is a toy for nimbler kids over seven. The ancestor of the Swiss Army Knife, the Blunt Stick is mega multi-functional. Is it a hockey stick, a golf club, a baseball bat, a fishing rod, or a javelin? All of the above, sports star. It's also a light-saber for a young Jedi knight. It's a sword, if your youngster wants to get medieval on another kid's ass. (Please note: I endorse chivalry and theatre, not bullying.) It's a baton for your future gymnast, and, for the big-boned child, it's a trusty roaster of marshmallows. (Oh wait, that's the Sharp Stick, never mind.) Best of all, the Blunt Stick is eco-friendly, as long as you don't snap it from the endangered St. Helena Gumwood.

3. The Empty Pill Bottle with Macaroni Inside. Note: I said macaroni, not pills. Take an empty, plastic pill bottle—preferably one of those chunky, bulk-size vitamin jars—and toss in a few rotini. Whatcha got? Instant maracas! Shake that baby booty! I recommend making a new label for the bottle so others don't think your kid's toy box doubles as a medicine cabinet.

4. The Wooden Spoon. A mere spoon? To the sadly unimaginative, perhaps. This common kitchen utensil is actually a magic wand. Seriously. Bang anything with it and that thing magically transforms into a drum. Throw in a stainless steel mixing bowl and it's a percussionist's starter set. At Long and McQuade, something like this would cost major coin. But lucky for you, the

elves that live in your cupboard dish out this playtime fun for free. Comes with free microphone setting.

5. The Pet Rock. A knockoff of the 70s fad. (Yes, this really was a huge novelty in that era. Probably on account of the rampant drug use.) Create your own twenty-first-century model by going no further than your own backyard, preferably un-landscaped. Fat ones or skinny ones, bumpy ones or smooth ones, sedimentary or igneous, your child can choose the pet that he or she wants, not necessarily the one that doesn't shed. *Disclaimer: If you live in a glass house, get a cat.*

6. The Empty Paper Towel Roll. There's pirate treasure on your countertop, between your toaster and your microwave. When the last paper towel is pulled from the roll—BAM—you got yourself a telescope, matey. Arrrrrgh you ready to sail the high seas of awesomesauce? For a *miniature* telescope, head on over to the bathroom.

7. The Imaginary Friend. The success of this toy depends on your level of commitment. Start talking to the empty space next to your child. For example, when I first asked Max, "Would you like to read a book?" I then moved my head twenty degrees to the right or left and asked the same question again: "And how about you?" At first, Max looked confused. But within days he started to realize—there *is* someone there. A friend! In two to three weeks, your child will be enjoying the constant companionship of a kid you never actually have to feed. Or give birth to.

Hide and Seek for Dummies

We play a lot of hide and seek at our house.

With the exception of hiding behind the couch to chinch his shorts with hot shit, Max sucks at this age-old game.

He is the worst hider in the history of the world.

He is on America's Most *Found* List.

If he had been a part of Al-Qaeda, Osama Bin Laden would

have Bin Gotten on September 12th.

Here is how it usually goes. I stay in the living room and start counting to ten while Max scurries excitedly down the hall. I get to eight…nine…nine and a half…nine and three-quarters…and I can still hear him running around from bedroom to bedroom, giggling.

So I shout, "Ready or not, here I come!" and start giant-stepping down the hall so he can hear my approach and make last-minute adjustments to his cloak of invisibility.

Clearly his cloak needs mending. I walk into his bedroom pretending not to see what's right in front of me. He's standing there holding a pillow up to cover his face. I prolong the game for at least a few seconds, seeing as we came all this way.

"Hmmm, what's this strange pillow-top statue doing here? And why is it wearing Max's tractor jammies? Imposter!"

Muffled giggling.

"Wait a second…. This faceless, pajama'd statue with feet is laughing! It's…it's…it's *alive!*"

His arms go weak with laughter and he drops the pillow.

"There you are. I knew it was you!"

This is progress. Sometimes he doesn't even apply the pillow. He just stands there with his eyes closed, because obviously I can't see him if he can't see me. Perfect logic. Did you know Max served on the jury for the Casey Anthony murder trial?

Occasionally he does find a good hiding spot, with Daddy's help. I see him right away, of course: in the clothes hamper, behind the door, or playing a CSI cadaver under the bedspread.

"Where's Max?" I inquire exaggeratedly.

If he doesn't start laughing right away, he immediately announces, "I'm right here!"

"Oh thank heaven, I thought you were lost to me forever."

I have not been this fake since I was eighteen and pretending to be legal drinking age.

If his hiding skills don't improve, he'll be grounded for the duration of his teenage life. And whatever will I do with all that poorly-stashed weed? Hmmm.

Kids just can't keep a secret. I remember spending the day with my nephews many years ago, when Max was but a pipe dream. (You know, from his daddy's pipe.) Glenn—my brother and dad to Jack, then six, and Sam, then three—was working offshore at the time. It was the day before Mother's Day, so I took the boys to the store to buy a card and some flowers for their mom. On the way home, I coached them on the art of discretion.

"Now guys, remember. This gift is a secret. You need to hide it when you get home and give it to your mom tomorrow. Not today. Tomorrow. Mother's Day."

Oh yes, they assured me. It was top secret. Classified. Mum's the word.

We walked into the house and Peggy, my SIL, was there to greet us.

"What did you do today?" She was eager to hear how the boys enjoyed their day with crazy Aunt Vicki.

Sam's gums were flapping before the front door was closed behind us. I shot lasers at him with my eyes but it was too late.

"We had fun," said Sam. "And we definitely did *not* buy you a card and flowers."

It's safe to say Sam will never be in the CIA.

Kids. They make terrible secret agents, criminals, and witnesses. Take this recent supper conversation:

"What did you do at daycare today, Max?"

"Play outdoors," he says.

"In the rain?"

"Uh-huh."

"Did you get wet?"

"Uh-huh."

"And did you also stay dry?"

"Uh-huh."

"So glad you had a great day, Houdini."

Guys and Dolls

When I first saw Max on the ultrasound all curled up in my uterus, he looked like a driver in the cockpit of a Formula One racecar. Of course he did. He exploded out of the gate. And from that moment on, he was all cars and trucks and tools and dirt. One of his first words was *vroom*,[4] and he was just seven or eight months old when he started driving a toy car up the arm of the sofa. Who taught him that? Not I. Not anyone. He's all snakes and snails and puppy dog tails, and backhoes and loaders and hammers and nails.

Driving past a construction site one evening, Max said, quite matter-of-factly, "Mom, when I gets a big boy, I'ma drive a cement truck and a dump truck and a steamroller. And when I gets a big boy, I'ma say 'fuck'." Now he says he's going to be a firefighter. Probably one that says, "Fuck. Fuck that fire."

He is all boy. Every time he wears his denim overalls, I expect a frog to jump out of the front pocket. Let's face it. It's only a matter of time before he starts watching TV with his hand down the front of his pants.

His favourite TV show is *Care Bears*. NOT. His favourites are *Bob the Builder*, *Mighty Machines*, and *Thomas the Tank Engine*. That's what gets Max's motor running. Oddly though, one of his favourite movies is *Gnomeo and Juliet*. An animated version of the most famous love story of all time, starring garden gnomes instead of people. Of course, as soon as I press play, Max demands, "Fight! Fight!" He wants me to fast-forward to the part where two gnomes, "both alike in dignity,"[5] try to run each other over with lawnmowers.

But Turbo Ginger is not entirely composed of jet fuel. He likes other things too. Like books! He loves books. In fact, he often asks if we can go to "Tractors." (He means Chapters.) When we get there, he beelines past the thousands of books to get to the train table. What books?

He does like to read though, I swear. He also likes making crafts,

[4] Right after that word, I taught him to say onomatopoeia.
[5] When it comes to Shakespeare, I'm a real gnome-it-all. Gnot really.

baking, playing with clay, finger-painting, puppet shows, and smelling babies. He has a tender, thoughtful, nurturing side. He cried when I read him *The Giving Tree*. "Why did the tree be a stump?" he asked, wiping his eyes with the front of his flannel pajama shirt. He also welled up when Sparky got hit by a car in *Frankenweenie*. Lips wriggling, he asked, "Why did Sparky get died?" My Turbo Ginger has a motor, and a big, beautiful heart.

Believe it or not, he also likes pink. Or, at least, he has no qualms with it. He sees no fault in fuchsia. Puce does not make him puke. He has no quarrel with coral. And he will happily drink from a pink cup. Dolls, purses, makeup—it's all good in this boy's world.

One day when I was at work, his pesky aunts put him in a princess dress and sent me a photo of my little Snow White eating an ice-cream cone, his reward for compliance. They said Max didn't even need to be bribed; he was game for giving the gown a whirl. It's not that he chooses these things, mind you. When given the option, he invariably picks the blue over the pink, the truck over the doll. He likes what he likes and chooses accordingly. But he doesn't vociferously reject the pink and the doll or recoil from it likes it's a bag of deadly viruses. And that's a big deal. Why would he reject it profusely? Is it really so horrible to like something typically enjoyed by the girls? Are we really so repulsive?

I'm careful not to subscribe to the "pink is for girls" bullshit. When I open the cupboard to a sea of coloured cups, I don't pick the blue cup because Max is a boy. In fact, I'm inclined to choose the pink cup. And no, ignoramus, I am not trying to turn my kid gay, even though it would be bloody fabulous to have someone in the family to tell me honestly how my ass looks in these pants. Newsflash: I don't have the power to alter his chromosomes. Pouring milk into a pink cup is not going to change his DNA. And even if it could, that's not why I choose the pink cup. I choose the pink cup to ignore the fucking ridiculous polarization of "boy stuff" and "girl stuff." Pink for girls only? Hells to the no. It's all made up. Just think about this for a second, please. Pink: a hue somewhere between red and magenta. The colour of pigs, cotton candy, and sunsets. As recent as the 1920s, pink was for baby *boys*— GASP![6] This is for realsies. Look it up. And look at the great and beloved Newfoundland Tricolour flag from the late 1800s. It's one-third pink! Will flying that flag make you one-third fag?[7] And if pink is so weak, why'd we go and name some deadly shears after it? Huh? Huh? No one debated the unmanliness of all this pink stuff, because pink was just a great colour—for everyone!

I blame the toy people, making toys for girls and toys for boys in completely separate plants, in completely separate cities.[8] I also blame Victoria's Secret and their motley "Pink" loungewear line. I blame flamingos. And I blame the English for making "pink" slang for "vagina." Go home, English people, you're drunk.

Long story short: I will not condone the insanity by choosing the blue cup. Unfortunately, the majority of parents do choose the blue cup. They don't even think about it. They're so immersed in the world's make-believe rules about gender and colour, their brains have stopped working. Some moms don't want to challenge the status quo because that would require feminist thinking, and as we all know believing in equality for women makes you grow a big giant beef whistle. They go right for the blue cup. Because boy equals blue. Game over. The end.

I wish it were the end, but it's only getting worse. They just came out with pink Legos. Pink ones. As if the blue and red and yellow and green bricks weren't for girls all along. And thanks for the "Friends" theme too, Lego. Obviously we gals don't want to build fire trucks or dinosaurs. We just want curvy little Lego chicks with pink and purple houses to decorate and pink and purple beauty shops to visit. Should we bake a pink and purple Lego pie too, maybe bring it over to the guys (no girls allowed!) at the Lego City Search

---

[6] In 1927, *Time* magazine printed a chart showing sex-appropriate colours for boys and girls according to leading US stores. In Boston, Filene's told parents to dress boys in pink. Don't believe me? Smithsonianmag.com/arts-culture/When-Did-Girls-Start-Wearing-Pink.html

[7] Forgive me, gay lovelies. Sometimes a bitch just gotta rhyme.

[8] I'm making this up, but you get the point: segregation, polarization, boys over here, girls over there.

and Rescue Centre? Maybe we can let them look up our skirts while we're there.[9]

Girls really get the shaft in the toy department. And it's making the one-dimensional image of girls worse. With toy manufacturers depicting us as homemaking, hair-styling, suburban, pink freaks, it's no wonder boys think we're weak. I solemnly swear if I ever hear Max say, "Don't be such a girl," or any variation on this statement, his punishment will be severe. Solitary confinement, tar and feathering, or—worst of all—no more popsicles. "Don't be such a girl" implies that being a girl is bad. It's contempt. And we all know what contempt leads to: violence. Oh, you're such a girl. How yucky! How horrible! People, with all the rape happening these days, maybe we should be teaching our boys how cool it is to be a girl, how girls and boys are more alike than different, and how we should maybe, oh I don't know, stop raping them? And maybe after the rape thing is nipped in the bud, we can start paying them fairly, and stop giving them such a hard time about their bodies. Just a suggestion. Maybe someone could pass my thoughts on to the men who make all the decisions? Okay thanks.

What's so wrong with letting our sons play with "girl stuff" anyways? Oh right, because dolls make boys gay. I suppose Richard Simmons would have been a womanizing pro wrestler with testosterone oozing from his tight curls if his mom hadn't let him play with Barbies. I didn't realize Barbie could reprogram your nucleotide sequences. And here I was thinking she was a dumb blonde; that bitch is a magician.

Yes, keep the dolls away, parents. Not only might it turn your son into a flaming homosexual; it might also make him a good father. Let's not let that happen, for Christ's sake. Let's keep the women in the kitchen pureeing the baby food and the men in the garage shining their weapons for the battlefield.

See, boys are getting the shaft in the toy department too. With no dolls on "the boy side" of the store and drone-like parents never

<hr>

[9] All but one of the Lego "Friends" wears a short skirt, as all girls should. At least the one in the pants is the redhead. Small victories.

questioning the way the world is laid out for them by marketing dicks, we're doing our sons a disservice. Of course there are no dolls for the boys. I mean, a replica of a small child to be held and changed and fed by a little boy who might be a dad someday? That's just absurd. Give this child a sword!

This is not *Leave It to Beaver*. The world has changed. Dad is folding the laundry and feeding the baby and frying the bacon that Mom just brought home. Or maybe he's doing all these things because Mom didn't come home at all, because there is no mom, or she lives on the other side of town. When it comes to the modern family, anything goes. There is no normal. But no matter what the family looks like, no matter how it's shaped, every kid needs the same thing: nurturing. So if you think you're doing your son a favour by protecting him from dolls that make him weak and gay and—god forbid—tender, you're actually screwing him over.[10] You're feeding the perception that nurturing is Mom's job. You know it's true that when parents separate, the mom is almost always the favourite in the eyes of the court, sometimes even when she's a total train wreck with a cocaine moustache. Why does Mom get the edge? Because the kid came out of her body? Because she's the soft, squishy one? As a feminist who hates that men rule the world, a little part of me enjoys that we get the advantage in at least one department. But as a feminist who wants men and women to be equal in every way, this is just not fair. Max might have kids of his own one day. It makes me sad to think that my wonderful son might not get the time he deserves with his children. They'll arrest me for contempt of court, for standing up and shouting, "But he drinks out of a pink cup! He has a doll!" I would do it. You know I would.

His name is Dustin Nolan, the Cabbage Patch Kid I gave Max for his second Christmas. He ripped off the gift wrap and gave Dustin a once-over like he was scanning for motors, wheels, switches, and levers. Within the hour, poor Dustin was face down in the dog dish. It was too late for CPR (Cabbage Patch Resuscitation). But he

---

[10] Research shows that spending time bonding with their babies lowers men's testosterone (and aggression) levels. Google the Aka tribe of Africa. Fathers there even let the babies suck on their nipples to pacify them...while the women hunt!

is still in Max's toy box, having survived several toy purges and trips to the Salvation Army donation centre. He doesn't come out to play much, but he often gets a role in the bedtime puppet show. Mostly he just lies there face down in the toy box, his powder-fresh sutured buttocks sticking up from a sea of superheroes and monster trucks. But his presence there is an important message. It's perfectly okay to have a doll in your big blue toy box.

Knowing the world is laid out for my son in every shade of blue and all kinds of fucked up, it's on me to make sure he understands that blue is for all of us. And so is pink. And so are Legos, and sparkles, and tractors, and dolls. No matter what the people around us have been hypnotized into thinking, everything is for everyone. I will keep pouring his juice into a pink cup as long as I can, because pink is just a colour, and a cup is just a cup. I will keep showing him, in as many ways as I possibly can, that the world is his oyster. And he can harvest the pearl with a hockey stick or a princess wand. Whatever he wants to do.

Mum mum mum mum mummy mummy mummy Lois…Hi.

— STEWIE, *THE FAMILY GUY*

CHAPTER FIVE

Turbo Ginger

[**turr**-boh-**jin**-jer] noun 1 a child with red hair, excessive energy, and fiery disposition. Also known as Gung-ho Ginger, Ginja Ninja, or Red Menace. 2 Not to be confused with Cranky Pants, Turbo Ginger is full of life, emotion, and awesomesauce. 3 The most famous Turbo Ginger who ever lived: Chuck Norris. Chuck Norris actually *chose* his ginger genes. Because even when it comes to DNA, Chuck Norris gets whatever the fuck he wants. 4 Also not to be confused with the reverse: Ginger Turbo. (Don't google it; you'll regret it.)

All that energy and emotion often manifests itself in the form of Trouble, with a capital T. These are the stories you will hear. But please note: my Turbo Ginger also does good things. Lots of good things. But come on, do you really want to hear about the three new words he learned today, or how cute his poop is, or where I got pull-ups on sale, or how amazing my life is? Exactly. This is entertainment, people. This is comedy. And comedy is pain.

Turbo Gingers: Born Not Made

Max is such a good boy. But turn your head for half a second and he's halfway to the Falklands in a stolen outboard motorboat.

A couple nights ago, we went throwing rocks in a pond—the poor Newfoundlander's equivalent of SeaWorld. A thousand rocks would not have been enough for our lil' stone slinger. We had to drag him home. Literally. And I've never meant literally more literally. We used the dog leash. Splash trotted home beside us, unrestrained. Luckily, Max thought being lassoed was kind of fun. (Sicko.) Otherwise, we would have had to do things the hard way. We carry a roll of duct tape with us for emergency tantrums.

Maybe it's a toddler thing. Terrible twos and all that.

Maybe it's a boy thing. Testosterone and stuff.

Valid arguments. But I'm not buying any of it.

This is the essence of the Turbo Ginger. Feisty, strong-willed, and built like a brick shithouse. From day freakin' one. On the day Max was born, the pediatrician wrote "hulk" on his chart. Well, what he actually wrote was "excellent tone," but he wasn't talking about his singing voice. Max came out flexin'. He came into the world like the Incredible Hulk bursting out of his purple pants. His first superhero task: destroy a sascrotch.

But we had no idea just what we were dealing with because the carrots had not yet sprouted. The fires had not yet been stirred. Once we saw the copper cast—the ginge tinge—emerging from his scalp, it all started to make sense. Put the Ritalin back on the shelf. Cancel the toddler therapy. We didn't have ourselves a lunatic. We just had ourselves…a ginger.

Travelling with Satan's Spawn

Thinking about flying with a toddler? Seven words: Don't sit next to the emergency exit. You might just use it.

I don't mean that. I mean, in the grand scheme of a two-week vacation, the four-hour flight there and back is just a fart in the pants. You can do it! But be forewarned. And pack at least six kinds of crackers. And a couple Valium for yourself.

Children under the age of two can fly for free. In Canada, at least. So, as new parents, we think, *Yippee! We'll take a trip somewhere before the half-pint is two. Give him a ride on a big ol' jet airliner—for free!* Not so fast, opportunistic little mama. Think this through. If it's relaxation you seek, you might want to consider leaving the Savage Patch Kid at home. There won't be much time for kicking your feet up. The kicking (and screaming) will be done by he who came from your V.

The drama begins at the airport. For the love of lemon gin, take your stroller. A toddler on the loose at the airport? You may as well post an ad on Kijiji: "One toddler for the taking. Likes cheese puffs, marshmallows, and long walks on the beach." You can push the stroller right up to the door of the airplane. Leave it there and board the plane; the stroller is magically waiting for you on the other side. But don't get too excited. The nightmare occurs in between.

Our flight to Ontario would have gone much differently had Max been a nine-month-old crawler instead of a sixteen-month-old Olympic sprinter. With a perfectly immobile baby on my lap, my biggest worry would have been keeping his ears clear and his belly full. I could have flicked on the cartoons, stuck a bottle in his gob, and giddy-up—vacation, here we come. But Max had learned to motor and had been honing his legwork for the past five months. Now he was bringing those mad skills onboard. No amount of *Thomas the Tank Engine* was going to stop him from busting a move on that Boeing 737. In fact, Thomas probably just reminded him to go full steam ahead. Damn you, Thomas, damn you.

For Max, boarding the plane was like walking into a new world of possibilities. His eyes lit up when he saw the endless rows of seats, each containing a different face. I could almost hear his thoughts, spoken in an English Stewie Griffin accent, of course:

What is this? A life-size Fisher Price Shake-n-Go Flyer? Oh goody! Must…explore…now. Check out the giant porn stash on that dude. Feast your eyes on that chick's big dangly earrings!

Can I grab them, Mommy? Can I? Can I? Oooooh, this little window shade is fun! It's open, it's closed, it's open, it's closed....

When we took our seats, we were pleasantly surprised to have been assigned the row with extra legroom. Bless your heart, travel agent lady. At least you tried.

I'm no dummy; I came prepared. I packed several *new* dinkies and toys. They worked—for a while. Eventually, Max started tossing everything to the floor. Half the time, the toy would wind up under someone else's seat, so I'd have to retrieve it with my head in a stranger's crotch.

"Excuse me, sir, could you move your undercarriage so I can find my son's train?"

I got a whiff of sweaty scrotum at least twice.

I also packed snacks galore. My purse was a vending machine: raisins, fruit, Cheerios, Goldfish crackers, porkchops, and a few sugary sweet treats for emergencies. But there were not enough snacks in the world to keep our boisterous boy down. By the time they had switched off the seatbelt sign, Max had turned on the Turbo Ginger.

We made the mistake of travelling at night. The flight left at 7 p.m., so I thought, *Perfect. He'll get on board in his PJs, have a bottle, then go to sleep...and Mommy and Daddy will watch a movie!* I am a stupid, stupid woman. Max was tired, but he fought it with every fiber of his twenty-five-pound being. And how could I blame him? This was an exciting new place. There was no crib, no darkness, no familiar surroundings. It couldn't possibly be bedtime! Damn that kid is observant.

He tried to escape our two-seat row, but Andrew's leg served as a barricade. It's not safe out there in the aisle! Some parents walk their kids back and forth to let them blow off steam. But this could easily go awry. People have hot beverages, and there's always a pretzel-wielding flight attendant coming or going. Besides, if I gave Max an inch, or ten feet of aisle, he'd take a mile. And that mile ends on a cirrus cloud (yes, those are the skinny ones) 30,000 feet above the ground. One glimpse of the buffet of faces beyond our row and things would get real ugly real fast. Try returning to our seat once he had a gander of that sweet action. Max Murphy Meltdown imminent.

Thankfully, he was content to stay in the one-foot by two-foot playroom in the sky (i.e., the space between the window and the aisle, minus the space taken up by mine and Andrew's legs). He flashed greasy grins at the gentleman across the aisle. He shook his baby booty. He was deliriously tired, lying on the floor for a few seconds as if he was going to go to sleep, then suddenly springing to life and cackling like Pinhead from *Hellraiser*.

Sometimes he'd lie there for a few extra moments and we'd get our hopes up—a ceasefire might just be near—when suddenly I'd feel little teeth chomping into my foot. What the…? Andrew and I cracked up with laughter. Until we cracked. Three hours into the journey, we were desperately begging the sandman to arrive.

Max slept for the last hour of the flight. Just enough time for Andrew and I to fall asleep. Then *ding ding*. Buckle your seatbelts, we're coming in for a landing. Fuck. Me.

The return flight was even worse. It was the red-eye; need I say more? (And need I crack a ginger joke?) This time, we even had a spare seat between us. A blessing? You would think so, wouldn't you? Mastermind Max only utilized this luxury for his lunacy. He stood up on the seat and threw things over the top at the poor people dozing behind us. A die-cast locomotive to the face leaves a mark.

My recommendation? Fly with your under-two-year-old before he or she is walking. If it's too late for that, travel with a partner whose first name is Saint. Don't fly at night unless you have the patience of Job and an IV of caffeine. If you have money to burn, buy the kid his own seat and attach your car-seat to it. (Apparently stapling his sleepers to the seat is a no-no.) If your mini human has miraculously developed the faculty of reason ("If you sit down and be a good boy, Mommy will give you a marshmallow") then lucky you. Or if you were blessed with a naturally chill child, congratulations, and you make me sick.

A Word from the Snottery

Andrew and I make a great team. One of us holds down Turbo Ginger's flailing limbs while the other one squirts pretty, pink antibiotics into his mouth.

"Here ya go, buddy, take the yummy medicine and make your ears *all* better."

THWAPP!

He smacks the syringe out of my hand with a jerk of frustration.

We both silently hold one another's gaze for a moment. He knows he just messed up. The wrath of Mother Ginger is coming.

"Okay, that's it ya little bugger. Open up."

I snatch the syringe out of the dog's mouth.

Legs kick, arms punch the air, copper curls swirl with pint-sized insanity.

"Daddy!"

I call in the reinforcements.

"Holy crap, he's squirmy."

"And strong! Hurry up and get it in there."

"That's what she said."

"Focus!"

"He's fighting me with his tongue."

"Ouch, he bit me!"

Fuck.

"Okay, five mls, we're done."

"Now, see, that wasn't so bad, was it buddy?"

The wild billy goat is free. Tears dry up instantly. Peace resumes. High five, honey! Meet you here in four hours for another rumble with Rainman. Oddly, Max has not yet discovered that he could actually spit the medicine out instead of swallowing it. Kids are so dumb.

Sometimes he takes the syringe and drinks it like it's liquid candy: mmmmm, bubble gum. But if he's not in the mood, he'll flick that gadget at your pupil quicker than you can say penicillin. Hence the need for force. We'll traumatize him with our aggressive methods, but hey, at least his ears will work.

I used to silently judge people whose kids were always sick. I mean clearly it was because their kids ate nothing but hot dogs and chicken nuggets or because their house was rotten dirty. But now I see the snot-nosed truth. Every kid is a cesspool of disease and infestation. A towering kettle of snot ready to explode at any given moment. The reason the Kleenex people are filthy stinkin' rich.

Max is a pretty healthy boy. When he gets sick, he's tough about it. Even with boogers flying, he's still motorin' (and wiping his nose-goo on the couch). But he has had a few ailments since I went back to work, when I released him into the big, scary world beyond my ample (*not*) bosom.

He has rocked the pinkeye. Apparently that's caused when you get poop in your eye. And there's no shortage of that around these parts. Pinkeye is super contagious, so of course I contracted it from the little bastard. I quarantined myself in my office at work and kept my head down to go to the bathroom. I knew they were looking at me and whispering, "I bet she got poop in her eye."

He has sported a polka-dot rash on his belly. The doctor took one look and said, "roseola." Rosy what? It was four in the morning and I was delirious. All I could think was: *What the hell is roseola, and aww that's a pretty word, I'ma name my next child Roseola.*

He's had the croup with that distinct seal-like bark—a sound so loud and startling, I caught sight of someone lurking in the bushes outside the house wielding a club and a rifle.

And he's had an ear infection—twice. The second time, his eardrum ruptured. Bloody ear gunk trickled out of his ear for two days. One day, he will use this incident as an excuse for not hearing me say, "Put away the iPad and eat your cauliflower!"

I'd like to think I'm keeping my boy as germ-free as possible. He loves broccoli, Brussels sprouts, and fish. Good immunity-boosting foods, I reckon. I mean, sure he has his treats and the occasional heaping pile of Kraft Dinner. And seriously, what kind of mother would I be if I didn't let him lick the icing off the beaters? It's a rite of passage, mandatory in my books.

I blow the dirt off the fork when it hits the floor; if there's a sink or a wet rag nearby, I might even rinse it off.

I dress him nice and warm so he doesn't catch a chill.

And I try and keep him away from other kids who are snottin' and barkin' and spreading their cooties. Which is virtually impossible because there is always at least one kid in the room who is clearly an expert in boogerology. I once saw a little girl with her hair stuck to her face on both sides with what one might call "homemade glue." I almost tossed my cookies.

I can't keep my munchkin in a bubble. And even if I could, I wouldn't. He needs to be around people, even other three-foot pillars of phlegm. Besides, not all germs are bad. Yogurt *is* bacteria! So there. And some bacteria found in our ears and mouths actually protect us from invading pathogens. I know this because I am a microbiologist in my spare time.

Colds and ear infections and this-ola and that-itis. It's all a part of childhood. Nature's way of armouring our little soldiers for life. We just do the best we can to keep them healthy, roll with the punches, and pray to the snot gods it's snot anything serious.

A Walking Nightmare

It's amazing how a simple stroll can morph into the hike from Hades.

It began flawlessly. A beautiful, dry, sunny winter day. The trails near Nanny and Poppy's pad in the Pearl[1] begged to be traipsed; days like these must be savoured. So we all got ready to hit the path: Poppy, Auntie Kim (visiting from Montreal), Uncle Chris (visiting from Vancouver), cousin Aidan, Mama (moi), Splash (ruff ruff), and Mad Max Murphy, who was about to live up to his nickname.

Max held Aunt Kim's hand and marched along beside her, so happy to be in this magical place they call the outdoors. I thought, *okay, we can do this.* But I felt a twinge of dread as I watched Andrew drive off moments earlier with the stroller peeking out the window of the hatchback. Dear, sweet stroller with glorious seatbelt that securely contains ornery offspring.

---

[1] Mount Pearl is Newfoundland and Labrador's third largest city and home of the Glacier, Tol's Time-Out Lounge, and the most cougars per capita on Canada's east coast.

The first three minutes of our excursion went splendidly. Cool breeze. Bright sun. Well-behaved son.

And then…

Mr. Independence showed up. He didn't need to hold anybody's hand. Holding hands was for babies! I mean, come on, he had been walking now for like nine whole months; he had this walking shit down pat, yo. So step off, motherfuckers. He was the envy of crawlers everywhere.

Okay, fine, so no handholding. But he insisted on walking off the pavement of the trails and into the grass beside it, which just so happens to be where every piece of broken glass and dog turd is hiding, waiting for an unsuspecting shoe.

We tried to redirect him to the beaten path, but then he decided he would try out the other side of the trail—the downward sloping side that tumbles into a babbling brook full of jagged rocks and green slime. Excellent.

I'm all for letting him do his thing and acquire a couple bumps and bruises which my grandfather would have affectionately called "larnin,"[2] but we simply couldn't let the little frolicker out of our grasp here. If he tumbled over the slope, unable to control his momentum, he'd end up face-first in the stream with a rock in one nostril, a tiny fish in the other, and his two front teeth in his back pocket.

I had started out chilly, wishing I had brought along my hat and mittens. By now, just ten minutes in, I was sweating, and cursing Andrew for driving off with the sacred stroller. But I mustered up my courage and trudged on, this time holding the hood of Max's coat to try and steer him in the direction of the rest of the Murphy pack, or at least away from certain death. But no go; if we were walking *this* way, Max was running *that* way. And I swear, if I stood there and let him go, waving my hand and saying, "Bye-bye, Max," he'd just keep on going. I tried it, several times. Does he look back? Sure. And then he chuckles, flashing every little tooth in his head, and keeps on truckin'. If I could read his mind,

---

[2] Learning. In this case, by experience. I miss my pop.

he'd be shouting "Freeeeeeedom!" My little William Wallace. My little reason to drink wine straight from the bottle.

Then things took a turn for the worse. Puddles. It had rained a lot just a couple of days earlier, depositing pools of water in every darn dent in the asphalt. Max's socks and shoes were wet within seconds. That's all we needed, to start the new year off with pneumonia. We tried everything to divert his attention. But as soon as I'd attempt to guide him in another direction, he'd fall to the ground in a wiry heap. Next he'd be face and eyes in a big, cold puddle, and that would just be gross. The only way to drag him away? Body and bones. Between myself and Chris, we made our way back to the house with Max kicking and screaming in our arms. He flicked off his sneakers, snatched my sunglasses, and grabbed at my earrings. There it was. The Ginger Snap. There was no going back now. I just needed to get Opie's[3] evil twin back to the house and into his cage.

When we finally reached the house, I ripped off his soaking shoes, socks, and pants and released him into the living room, still crying and flailing his arms. Within seconds, the diapered demon had snatched the remote controls off the coffee table and hurled them, one by one, over the stairs into the porch.

So. That was an enjoyable walk. Perhaps resembling the walk to the electric chair. Or a walk on red-hot coals en route to a cannibal feast where you are the main course. Or the walk toward a room with a door that reads, "Drug-free Childbirth."

He's in preschool now and things have vastly improved. One day he'll be able to walk sensibly beside me as I point out trees: "Look, that's a fir, like a Christmas tree!" And birds: "That's a Blue Jay, like the baseball team!" And other items in nature: "That's not a furry white rock, honey. Put that down."

One day, we'll read this together and laugh, maybe while he's holding my withered hand as we slowly walk along a trail behind the seniors home where he pays good money to keep me all locked up.

---

[3] If you know who Opie is, either you're a classic TV nerd or you bought this book with your pension cheque, and I thank you. Opie Taylor is the little boy from *The Andy Griffith Show*, played by Ron Howard.

Kids Are Really, Really Gross.
And Disgusting, Also

And that's a gross understatement.

One evening as I was tidying up the living room after Max went to bed—my riveting nightly ritual—I noticed a big gooey streak, about two inches long, across the couch. It was like a slug had slithered by, leaving behind its thick, yellowy ooze to say, "I was here, bitches." But I have never seen a slug inside our house (except my husband after a night out with the boys), and I doubted that this was the first sighting. No, this stripe of sticky spunk had the look of something emitted by a wet nostril. A tiny wet nostril on the face of a gorgeous yet gruesome kid who sees no difference between a Kleenex and Mama's new sectional sofa.

I never particularly like talking about bodily fluids. I mean, cum on, who does? But since I became a mother, it has become a part of my everyday vocab. Snot. Poop. Puke. Spit. Pee. Boogers. Earwax. Scabs. When people see me on the street, they think, *damn that bitch got it together*, but guaranteed, somewhere on my clothes is a little patch of crud that originated from some orifice of my son. How do you like me now?

Now I know he can't help it. He's still pretty new to the planet, still exploring the order of the universe. But still, he's a grody little explorer, ain't he? He sits there eating supper in his high chair with a giant noodle stuck to the side of his face. Now, how on earth does he not know that's there? This truly boggles my mind. Or maybe he does know and he just doesn't care. Same reason he doesn't give a shit that there's a pound of poop dangling between his legs and mashing into his butt cheeks when he sits.

I vividly recall a Sunday at the local pool. Oh the mayhem of getting us both out of wet clothes and into dry clothes with Max constantly running back toward the showers where we had just spent twenty-five minutes with a boogie board. (Yes, he'd rather stand in the shower than get in the pool.) So I whipped out the raisins to try and occupy him while I speed-dressed. He skipped around the change room with the teeny Sunmaid box, dropping raisins on the yucky wet floor and picking them up and eating them. Have you seen the floor of a swimming pool locker room? It's like the crap you yank out of your bathtub drain once a year: a soup of stale water and hair and toe jam and belly-button lint. Can you get athlete's foot in your mouth?

During his first visit to a beach—beautiful Windmill Bight on the northeast coast of Newfoundland—he ate about two cups of sand. I have pictures and witnesses to prove it. The proof was also in his poop that night. He basically shit cement.

He makes out with Splash—a lot. Seriously, he consumes at least a couple tablespoons of dog saliva daily. What am I supposed to do? He loves doggy kisses, and Splash loves searching the inside of his mouth for leftovers.

He eats bubbles. Like, those oily orbs that float around in the air with which every kid on earth is fascinated. At the Little Gym, at bubble time, he gets down on all fours and puts his mouth around bubbles that land on the floor without popping. It's a weird visual, let me tell you. Bursting the bubble with his finger like other kids is not enough for Curious Ginger; he has to eat the thing.

When he gets in the bathtub, he drinks the bath water. If there's no cup in the tub to scoop it up, he'll suck it out of a facecloth. And that's not the worst of the bathtub shenanigans, trust me. One Monday morning, he woke up at six (sigh), and my aunt Linda (Max's babysitter) wasn't picking him up until 8:45. So we had lots of time to get things accomplished: breakfast, play, maybe even a bath! I really should be less ambitious. Max was in the tub playing and splashing, so I left the bathroom for a minute to get dressed, then returned to the bathroom to de-uglify. I went right to the mirror over the sink without glancing toward the tub. I could hear him playing as usual; all was well. But then a whiff of something foul danced across my nose. I turned to see Max in the tub—with about ten little brown balls of excrement floating around him. I immediately plucked him from the chocolate milk, dried him off, and released him so I could try and clean up this horrendous crime scene. On the bright side, maybe this was potty training progress; the tub is right next to the toilet.

So I did a preliminary clean-up, knowing a more thorough disinfecting was going to be required, and walked out to the living room to check on my little shit disturber. He was standing there watching TV with a little puddle in front of him. Of course. He peed on the floor. I mean he couldn't have peed in the tub; that would have been *wrong*.

But wait, it gets better. I went back to the loo to spray the tub with disinfectant. Then I grabbed a diaper from his room. Hey, there was no rush to diaper him now that he had expelled everything in his system! But by the time I got back to the living room, he was standing there with a shocked look on his face, pointing to a spot on the floor about five feet away from him. I walked gingerly (shut your mouth) toward the spot that was hidden from my view by the coffee table, and there it was. Another steamer. I honestly wondered if it was doggy barf, but Splash hadn't budged from her spot under the highchair where she was waiting, shark-like, for the remnants of breakfast. It had to be Max. And sure enough, I found a smudge of the putrid evidence on his butt cheek when I carted him off to his change table to get diapered and dressed, but first—CORKED.

Just in case there wasn't enough shit back there…

Motherhood Is the Shit

The nurse comes into my room on the maternity floor.

"Did you eat a lot of fruit today?" she asks with a curious smile.

"Ummm, no?"

My three-day-old jaundiced son was in an incubator down the hall and Florence Frightengale here was talking about apples and oranges?

She chuckled. "Max just pooped and it shot right out of the hole in the side of the incubator."

Not connecting the dots? Fruit has fibre. Mommy eats fruit. Breastmilk transfers fibre to baby. Baby shoots supersonic, projectile

poop missiles.[4] Excellent work, son! Next time, point your cute little crap cannon right at the meany-faced nurse. You know the one. Get 'er right in the meany eye.

And so it began. My entire existence would henceforth revolve around the emissions of this child's itty-bitty bunghole.

During those six days at the hospital with my little munchkin with the excess bilirubin, I had to document every dang detail of his brownload downloads. Colour, frequency, size—it was a proper doo-doo diary. From black meconium to guacamole green to mustard yellow, his Crayola box of crappola indicated his bilirubin was regulating, his liver-tan was fading, and we could finally take him home. After a week-long impression of "50 Shades of Michael Jackson."

I stole as many diapers from the hospital as my duffle bag would hold and went on my merry mommy way.

Before long, Max's butt nuggets became that familiar shade of brown. Now that's the shit I know…and love? My romanticized notions of motherhood quickly kerplunked to the bottom of the diaper pail. Beyond the bliss of little white onesies and cloud-soft chenille blankets was the fundamental truth that we are all just animals, performing the most basic of human functions. Eat. Breathe. Shit. Sleep. Survive. Max and I, both.

In a twist of cruel irony, my dad was battling colon cancer. He had a tumour removed from his bowel the very day I peed on a stick and heard it scream, "Pregnant!" Good and bad, the colon was certainly seeing a lot of action in our family. But let's keep this light, shall we? Back to the ass goblins.

Shit was everywhere. Yes, fan included. If I had one of those super-cool infrared CSI poop detectors, there'd be one solitary white patch behind the fridge where shit had yet to splatter. But hey, we were home. Let the feces fall where it may.

It's when we ventured out into the real world that things got messy. More than once we stripped Maximus Stinkimus down in public places, including once in the parking lot of a car dealership as

---

[4] Actually, it doesn't work this way at all. But the nurse must have thought so. Clearly I was in excellent hands.

we shopped for a new ride. I triple-bagged his clothes as my husband dangled the fifteen-pounder out the car door. Max had shat himself from neck to knees. If I hadn't packed extra clothes for him, we would have had to wrap him up in a Pontiac poster. Stool-resistant seats blasted to the top of our "things we need in a car" list. Basically, we needed to drive Frank Barone's couch.

We were rolling with the punches of new parenthood, but this shit storm was a new climate for us. Two years prior, our new puppy had arrived, fully trained to poop in the yard at nine weeks old. Human babies are slow on the uptake. But fast on the download.

But I didn't realize just how wonderful infant poop was until Max, around age one, started depositing full-size, mega-toxic shitsicles. I may as well have been changing my husband's diaper. One day, honey. (Please god no.)

And around age two, the butt-munchkin started assuming "the position." Turbo Ginger never stops, so when he does it's either because *Thomas* is on Treehouse or there's a corn-eyed butt snake en route to Pantsville. Here's how it goes: I notice a sudden silence. This can only mean one of two things. He's either standing there across the room holding a pair of scissors and staring at me thinking, *Will she stop me, or shall I go ahead and carve the shit out of those curtains?* Or he's bent over at the waist at a forty-five-degree angle, red-faced and quivering, squeezing some Mississippi mud into his diaper like a human tube of toothpaste.

His body in a full Nazi salute, it's like he's a member of the Turd Reich. Okay, that's it. When my kid starts to remind me of Adolf Hitler, I know it's time for change. It's potty time, baby.

We didn't push the potty training too hard, warned by many that he might rebel and either get a tattoo or start pinching loaves all over the house. But once he realized what we were up to, Max started hiding. Behind the couch. Behind his bedroom door. And he started saying things like, "I gotta go see a man about a horse." Okay, that's a lie. But he did start saying, "I go hide," and, "Don't look at me." Oh okay, Mr. Mysterious, whatever could you be up to? You better not be smoking cigarettes in there or watching those skanks on *Toddlers & Tiaras.*

As I write this (which will be long before you read it, but whatever), he's almost three and about eighty-seven percent trained. He has the occasional accident, but who doesn't? (Blush.) The day is quickly approaching when I will no longer accidentally lick "chocolate" off my wrist, and I can buy more wine and less crap-catchers. Those friggers are fifty cents a poop, er, pop! I'm broke. And I'm not just talking about my vagina.

In the meantime, I'm savouring my little pooper's first life endeavour. (Well, second, if you count "latching on.") His determined, wide-eyed poop face is cute as hell, despite the assault on my nostrils as an ungodly aroma wafts up from below. He looks down through his legs to see the chalupas he's dropping and exclaims, "Look—it's poop!" No shit, Sherlock. He has pooped on the potty about seventy times now, and he's still psyched—every time. It's the gift that keeps on giving.

Then we "drop some friends off at the lake." Proud and excited, he watches it swirl down the drain and exclaims, "Bye poopy, see ya later!" I sure hope not, dude.

Rock-the-Boat Baby

We are an outdoorsy family. Well, it's mostly my husband. Truth be told, I prefer luxury hotel rooms, but my poverty and inner poet necessitate the camping/nature-loving lifestyle, so I go with it. To hell with worldly travels and gourmet meals; I have perfected the s'more, damn it! I can carve the perfect wiener-roasting stick! And I will poop in a bush if required, with a shit-load of wet wipes to erase all memory of it from both arse and hands.

The moment Max was born, my husband excitedly followed the nurses over to the table where they cleaned and weighed our gooey gift from the gods. He wanted to get a head-to-toe gander at his boy. He was, of course, sizing him up to see how big the lil' tyke's first lifejacket should be.

Andrew wisely delayed the purchase until Max was two, and we took our tot to a pond just a few minutes from the house. The evening was peaceful. The water was calm. But the twenty-minute canoe ride to come would be neither of these things.

When we got to the pond's edge, we kept Max locked securely in his car seat while we hoisted the boat off the roof of the car and unloaded all the gear. Otherwise, in about seventeen seconds, Max would have been up to his neck in pond scum with a fishhook in his nostril.

While Andrew dragged the canoe to the water, I took Max out of the car and got him into his new, bright yellow life vest. Excellent. No matter what mayhem was about to ensue, at least the little meatball would float, and choppers would spot him from above.

I had dressed him appropriately before we left the house. A wide brim hat, waterproof jacket, and camouflage rubber boots—so I wouldn't see the dirt on them later. And because camouflage is cool on people under the age of nine. After that, you're looking for trouble, Billy Jim Bob. "The flies were t'ousands," as grandfather would say. But according to the OFF! can, fly dope is not to be used on children twelve and under. Okay then. So we can start protecting our kids from mosquitoes around the same time we start protecting them from gonorrhea: "Max, I need to have a talk with you about the birds and the bees...and the nippers."[5]

Fine, no fly dope. I'm innovative. I attached five plastic frogs to Max's jacket and stapled a Venus Flytrap to the top of his hat. Ha ha, tricked ya now, ya little pesky bastards! I will be appearing on *Dragon's Den* with these inventions next season. As well as my prototype for a robot that picks up beer bottles and dirty socks, magically removes the ungodly stench from hockey equipment, and performs cunnilingus at the push of a button. Expect Android Andrew to be on the market by 2017.

We strategically placed ourselves in the boat: Daddy in the back, Mama in the front, and Max sitting on a little folding chair right in front of me where my hand was mere millimetres from the handle on the back of his life vest. So *that's* why they put that handle there! All this time I thought it was for hanging it to dry.

---

[5] A Newfoundland term to describe a mosquito. One time a nipper nipped me right on the nipple.

Drowning was not a concept Max had grasped yet. First, pooping in the toilet. Then, avoiding death. All in good time.

The chair worked for about five minutes. Then he started to get shifty. Of course. "Nobody puts Baby in a corner," and nobody puts Turbo Ginger in the bow.

Time for the art of distraction.

"Oh, look at the bird, Max! Oh, look at the pretty trees. Let's count them. One…two…forty-seven…. Oh, listen to the loon! And do you hear the quad ripping the shit out of the ecosystem across the way? Awesome."

My bullshit worked for about ninety seconds. Then he called my bluff and started grabbing at my paddle, which I'd been trying to keep out of his view from the get-go. I would have had to shove it up my ass to keep his eyes off it now.

I quickly gave in. I had no choice, really. He was flipping out, and with no naughty chair in sight except a watery grave for three, I let him hold the paddle. He slapped the water with it as gracefully as a crack-baby beaver slapping its tail. I kept my hand on the top of the handle. Until he noticed I was doing so. He would have none of my paddle-groping. Skipper Max Murphy could man this ship alone! So I let go and the heavy oar almost pulled him headlong into the pond. But it was okay; I had a ninja death grip on his life vest. Giving birth to this child was extremely painful and I wasn't about to do it over.

So the heavy oar escaped Max's puny pipes and he watched with horror as it drifted away…until Daddy reached out and grabbed it! Daddy, our hero! So we played this new game of Drop the Paddle, oh, seven or eight times, and as riveting as it was, it got old fast, especially when Max wouldn't let anyone else have a turn. Once, the paddle got away from Daddy's Elastigirly reach and we had to circle back around to retrieve it. The Love Boat soon ran out of fuel, and patience. Come on, Cap'n Stubby, it's time to head back to shore.

And by the way, all this time, as I struggled to keep Max of this world, with one hand on him and the other batting away flies as they harvested my delicious flesh, Daddy—our hero—was in the back of the boat fishing, footloose and fancy-free. I was trying to keep our little one in the boat, and he was trying to snag the big one. I prayed a 150-pound mud trout would emerge from the depths and swallow him whole. A good way to die in Andrew's books, I reckon. But not this day; I needed him to get us back to shore where safety and sanity awaited like a cold bottle of beer.

All We Need Is Just a Little Patience

Saint Augustine said, "Patience is the companion of wisdom." Bullshit, Gussy boy. What do you know anyway? You were the Bishop of Hippo! (True story. Hippo is in present-day Algeria.)

Ancient proverbs were meant to be changed. Patience is the companion of *pain*. For parents of toddlers anyways.

I often describe Max as the kind of kid who runs into oncoming traffic.

So of course when my aunt (the babysitter) takes him for a walk and he is the toddler from Baby Utopia, holding her hand and prancing calmly alongside her, she has to call and tell me about it. I know he's not all bad; he has his halo moments. And I was truly glad they were having such an amicable outing, mainly because I want her to keep minding the little bugger on the cheap. I said, "I'm so glad he's being such a good boy." My inner voice said, "Little fucker. He's saving the Turbo Ginger just for me."

So 5 p.m. finally arrived and I rushed home from work on this glorious spring day that just begged to be splattered in barbecue sauce. Max was in the backyard playing with Daddy and doggy. I handed Daddy the hamburger patties and he fired up the barbecue, leaving me to mind Max. But I needed to go to the store to get a couple extra things for supper. And I was starving, so I would have killed the last living panda bear to get to the place where they sell food in great quantities.

I tried to entice Max to come with me. "Wanna go to the store with Mama?"

Fake excitement fell on deaf ears on account of busy hands. He was holding a giant spade shovel, jabbing at the dusty horseshoe pit with all his mini might. To abandon this riveting work would be a fate worse than death. And that's how it almost played out as I carried him, body and bones and stark ravin' mad, back to the house to try and negotiate a plan to get my ravenous rump to the store. And by the way, leaving him in the backyard unsupervised was not an option; our backyard is a half-acre patch of grass carved out of some farmland surrounded by a moat of stinger nettles with a steep drop-off on one side that will land you among pointy alders and a secret village of evil dwarves. I had to go to the store, and he had to come with. No alternative.

ATTEMPT #1: "Hold Mama's hand and we'll walk to the store together. Maybe Mama will even buy you some Smarties over there!"

Shag the Smarties. No go. He was determined to get back to the shovel. He tried to rip his hand out of mine, and when I held on tight, he hit the ground in a helicopter spin, his head nearly smacking off the pavement. My further attempts to negotiate were futile; he was in Turbo Ginger mode and I was wasting my breath. So I dragged him into the house and plopped him in the naughty chair.

ATTEMPT #2: I told Andrew to get his tricycle. (It has a handle on the back that I push; his feet could barely touch the pedals.) "Ooooh Max, Daddy's getting your bike! Let's go to the store on your bike! Yay!"

His eyes lit up, tears receded like the Red Sea when Moses honed his mad skillz. Yessir, he took the bait. But twenty seconds later as we were approaching the bike, he tried to turn the tables. He didn't want to get on the bike; he wanted to *push* the fuckin' thing! But Short Stuff couldn't reach the handle, so that simply wasn't going to work. I tried to get him on the tricycle again. I even took off his helmet to see if that was half the problem. Yes, I was willing to sacrifice safety for sanity, and potato salad. But no sir. He kicked and screamed and I dragged him back into the house again, the bike abandoned at the edge of our country road. Back to the familiar spot: the naughty chair. (I should get a wooden chair and call it the knotty chair for added amusement. With a few disciplinary splinters.)

ATTEMPT #3: At this point I had resigned myself to *not* going to the store. Whatever we had in the fridge was a freakin' cornucopia of deliciousness right about now. But here he comes again, wiping his tears with a dirty sleeve.

"Store, Mama? Store, Mama?"

Okay sure, I'll try this one more time, Max. I bent down to his eye level and said, extra clear, "Now, are you gonna be a good boy and hold Mama's hand and never let go?"

Affirmative. We walked to the store without incident. We passed the neighbour's doggy and gave him a wave. We passed some ducks and practiced our quacking. We walked by a couple irresistible puddles and he didn't even try to jump in them. Could this be… sweet victory? At the store, I actually tried to let go of his hand a couple times in order to carry the groceries, but he would not let go for nothin'. In your face, Turbo Ginger. Mommy wins. Maybe I should try this patience thing more often.

He grabbed an orange out of the produce bin, his reward for being a good boy. And he could've had Smarties. Sucker.

Shopping Maul

So we arrive at the mall with no stroller. And now you know, with just one brief sentence, to which genre this story belongs. Let me Gibb it to you like this: "When the feeling's gone and you can't go on, it's *tragedy*."

When you venture into the world beyond your living room with a compact conniption fit waiting to happen, you need one of three things: a stroller, a leash, or a pet carrier with wheels. Pretty sure that last one is illegal. And even the leash is not my fave because it doesn't prevent the ol' Drop & Resist. (I'll explain later.) Basically, you need a straightjacket with wheels to keep things contained and moving forward.

Rental stroller it is. Let's do this.

So we shop around—la, la, la…whistle, whistle, whistle—life is good. We go to Winners and I tell Max he can have *one* thing. So he picks a *Thomas the Tank Engine* puzzle book. Wow—so surprised. But hey, this book claimed to improve cognitive skills and was under seven bucks. Excellent choice, son!

Yeah, yeah, I know. You shouldn't give your kid something every time you go to the store as he will come to expect it and then what's next—the world? I don't do that. I mean, not *every* time. Just most of the time. It's a small price to pay for my sanity for the next two hours, okay? I see it as a seven-dollar cover charge for entering the mall in the first place. I build the loss into my budget.

So we get in the checkout line that's a little too long under these toddler-toting circumstances. But he has his book; his patience will be rewarded. Suddenly Max lets the book slide to the floor and makes no effort to retrieve it. I know where this is going. Straight to Fucktown.

"Oops, you dropped your book there, buddy."

I picked it up and put it back in his lap. His grip on it was weak. He was having doubt. He was vulnerable. Oh god no, don't look around! The shelves around the checkout, of course, were loaded with crap, strategically placed there to mindfuck your life.

He sees it: a monster truck. "Want it, want it, want it."

Damn it, damn it, damn it.

"You can only have one thing, so do you want the truck or this awesome, amazing, stupendous book?"

"Truck."

Son of a…

Improves motor skills and…ten dollars? Shit. Okay, fine. If it means I can go to one more store in peace while he plays with this big-wheeled bastard, so be it.

So we paid for it and headed to Sears. About twenty minutes later, as I'm going through the Sears checkout, I notice the truck is gone.

"Where's your new truck, Max?"

Blank stare. He had no idea and didn't give a rat's ass.

The lady behind me overherd and said she saw a toy truck down in the slipper section. Yup. Here I was paying for slippers. Truck must have slipped right out of his hand. That can happen when you're in the slipper section.

Great, so he hated it already. Ten bucks up in smoke. I go back to the slipper aisle, find the truck, and place it back in his lap. He would have shown more excitement if I had handed him a potato.

Okay we were done here. Let's bring back the rental stroller and get the bejesus before naptime creeps up and bites me in the arse.

Too late. As I was taking all the stuff out of the rental stroller to carry by hand, Max started saying—no, *demanding*—"Thomas book! Thomas book!"

No way, Doris Day. He always does this. Picks one thing over the other and then changes his mind when it's too late.

A really lazy mother would have taken him back to the store and got the book, right? A smarter mother might have said, "Oh we'll go back and get that book, we just need to go to the car and get more money." And never go back, obviously. I am neither lazy nor smart. I simply explained that he had made his choice and we were going home now.

And then the ginger fever took hold. Crying. Stomping. And the symptoms were bound to get worse. I mustered up all my courage, took his hand, and beelined for the exit.

We had to walk the length of the mall to get to the exit where I had parked. It felt like the Boston Marathon. As we were passing through the main lobby, my disgruntled leprechaun kicked things up a notch with the ol' Drop & Resist. If you've ever had a kid, you know what this is. He plops down on the floor, refusing to go any further. I try and pull him along by the arm, but he throws himself backwards, making it virtually impossible to move him without looking like the mother from *Carrie*.

Very clever, children of the corn. And quite maddening. Max likes to add an extra twist by biting my hand to make me let go. Ever been bitten by your own kid? I know you have. And I know you had that split-second desire to punch them square in the face. But you didn't. Because you love your kid. Especially those little serrated teeth.

Oh, and we weren't just in the lobby with Saturday afternoon foot traffic comparable to Grand Central Station. We were also smack dab in front of a bunch of hot firefighters who had a kiosk set up there. Well that's just peachy. I chuckled and did an exaggerated eye-roll that said, "Kids…what are ya gonna do?" I had sweat dripping from my face, but I tried to keep my cool so they wouldn't have to use their hoses to put me out.

By the way, I should tell you—I would have thrown the scallywag over my shoulder and stomped out of there five minutes earlier had I been born an octopus instead of a fox. I had Max's backpack in my hand, and a bulky bag of new purchases. I was at capacity. Physically, and now mentally.

I did try to carry him along with all the stuff, but I just couldn't position Max in a way that prevented his feet and hands and teeth from maiming me. He was a shark trying to escape a fisherman's net. A shark with feet and hands.

So I tried to ignore him, as many mothers so kindly advise. But here's the thing: ignoring is definitely the most effective option at home, in the shopping cart at the grocery store, or even on foot in a more secluded area of a store. But in the busy lobby of the mall, it's a little more challenging. And yes, half of the challenge is my own embarrassment. People were looking at me, damn it! "Oh that poor girl with that savage of a child." I just wanted it all to end! And knowing my headstrong mini-me, we could be "ignoring" this episode for a good ten or fifteen minutes. (Some mornings, he won't let me get him ready for daycare so I put him in the naughty chair and he sits there for fifteen-plus minutes just staring at the wall. When asked if he is now ready to get dressed, he says no and goes back to sitting and staring. Maybe the naughty chair is a little too comfy.) Next time I resolved to hang tough for as long as it takes, no matter how many eyewitnesses.

I managed to drag him over to a bench. We were so close to the exit now. So very close. I could taste the asphalt and it was delicious. I just needed to gather myself together and prepare for the parking lot, where flailing gingers and hard pavement do not mix well. And why did I park so far from the door? I hate me.

En route to the bench, by the way, I saw my cousin and his new girlfriend. There was an on-the-fly introduction and they ran for their lives. He probably went straight home and hammered his nuts with a mallet.

I tried to sit Max on the bench, to get him to calm down a tad. There was no reasoning. The impenetrable wall of crazy was up and I was but a fetus with a slingshot. His arms were flailing, his teeth were gnawing, and my face was a bowl of sweat on the concrete floor. I think I saw a freckle float by.

A young father was sitting on the bench next to me with a little boy in a stroller. The kid leaned over the side of his stroller to look at the spectacle unfolding before him. His father looked astounded too.

"What? Like your kid is perfect! Look at him. He doesn't even have any hair and what is he—five? Get that kid a toupeé for Christ's sake!"

That's what I was thinking. What I said was: "Wanna trade?"

His silence meant no, I guess. Fine. Be that way, Caillou's dad.

The manager of a department store nearby was working near the store entrance and flashed me a couple understanding eyes. I love understanding eyes. If every person perfected that look, the crime rate would plummet. Of course, he would have *really* impressed me if he had offered to carry my bags to my car while I lugged my Tasmanian Devil. Asshole.

So I bit the bullet and grabbed everything—child, shopping bags (full of buyer's remorse), sweaty hog face—and headed for the parking lot. He was jammed under my arm like a sheep about to be sheared. When I got through the door, I set him down and dragged him by one arm across the parking lot, crying all the way. He was crying too.

We were almost at the car when he plopped down between two trucks, still saying "Thomas book" over and over until there's not enough wine in the world to erase the word from my mental chalkboard. I told him a big truck was coming and would squash him to a pulp if he didn't get in the car. He jumped up and took my hand, suddenly compliant. If that hadn't worked, I would have resorted to the age-old threat: "If you don't listen to Mommy, *the big man* is going to come and take you." Desperate measures.

There's a reason we feel that sense of dread when we enter the mall on Saturday afternoon with a toddler less than two hours from naptime. It's our body warning us: Abort! Abort! If we're going to risk going to the worst possible location at the worst possible time with the worst shopping companion in the universe, we must be prepared to laugh through the pandemonium that is sure as shit to ensue. The lineups. The tantrums. The hot fireman who might have imagined you sliding down his pole were you not sweating and wrestling with el diablo loco. Laugh at your crazy kid. Laugh at your own idiocy. Laugh at all those parents with their ten-month-olds sitting quietly in their strollers at the mall. Oh yeah. They're gonna get theirs.

Kids Are Assholes

My kid is an asshole. Scratch that (ass), let me rephrase. My kid has *asshole moments*. Hence the monikers I use for him when chronicling our misadventures: Red Menace, Savage Patch Kid, Demon Child, Evil Troll, and, of course, Satan. Better than calling him a fuckin' asshole, no?

And hence the costumes. For his first Halloween, I dressed him up as a lobster. Only because I couldn't find a Satan costume small enough. It did feel rather hellish though, when I lowered him into the pot of boiling water.

By his second Halloween, there was an itty-bitty Beelzebub getup hanging in the closet. I sup'd it up with some felt letters. On the front: "HELLUVA KID." On the back: "DROP IT LIKE IT'S HOT." He carried a little pitchfork too, which was just a really big regular fork. And a sippy cup that read, "HOT SAUCE."

Last Halloween, his third, he was Darth Vader—another theatrical tribute to my little dude's dark side. My husband kept saying, "Darth, I am your father." And I kept following it with, "Say that one more time and I'll skewer you with a light sabre."

My mom's not a fan of my Mephistophelian labels for her precious grandson, or the costumes from Hell's Stitchin'. She's more of the "children are angels let's put them in halos and Gap khakis" type. And she's not the only one; I got your "bad mommy" mail responses to my blog. Thanks?

But come on, people. Fiery hair with curls that twirl into horns, pointy little serrated teeth, and angry eyebrows that are each one-half of the ninth circle[6] of Dante's Hell? It should be illegal to *not* dress this kid up as Lucifer! Not just on Halloween but every bloody day. It's like having a kid born with a humpback and not dressing him up as Quasimodo. Or having a kid with one eye and not dressing him up as a pirate. That's just a total waste of deformity, man. "ARRGH ya finished with those Cheerios, me harty?" And how frugal—one eye-patch and you're done! Save your money for freak school.

But it's not really about Max's fiery looks. It's about his fiery spirit. His hotheaded personality—the source of his asshole moments. Next Halloween, I'm thinking I might skip the whole Satan routine, pick up some nude pantyhose and elastic, and suit him up as a giant sphincter.

"Oh, what a cute costume. Let me guess…a cinnamon bun?"

"Asshole."

"Jesus man, I was just trying to guess."

Every kid has asshole moments and the one who tore me a new one is no exception. What kind of person throws an entire plate of food on the floor because one (I repeat, *one*) kernel of corn snuck onto that sacred plastic surface by clinging to the underside of a pork chop like Spiderman under a getaway car? An asshole, that's who. Oh and by the way, he *likes* corn! Except on days when he decides corn is kryptonite.

We drove past an excavator (which he pronounced "ass invader") but I didn't see the damn thing, so Max went nutso. *Oh sorry about that, son. I was foolishly focusing on my driving. My bad. Ass invaders are my world.*

He went berserk when his ice cream melted too fast. *Okay, one second while I stop time whilst lowering the temperature of the great outdoors with my mind.*

He turned on the assholery when I wouldn't let him eat popcorn

---

6   In Dante's *Inferno*, Hell is divided into nine circles, the ninth circle being divided further into four rings. Satan sits in the last ring. The ninth circle is where the worst sinners are punished.

off the movie-theatre floor. *Oh okay, go ahead. Maybe later we can check under our seats for globs of bubble gum.*

He went bat-shit when teenagers at the park weren't coming over to play with him. *Step aside, perfectly reasonable son, while I ask these hoodlums to put out their cigarettes and play tag. Maybe you could also play connect-the-dots with their piercings.*

He threw a fit because there were four nuggets instead of the requested three. *Oh god no, not an EXTRA NUGGET. How dare these people be so generous? Let Mommy take care of that for you. Nom, nom, nom.*

He got upset because I wasn't looking at him. *So sorry I missed the 800th time you jumped a half-inch off the floor in an amazing feat of athleticism. This must be what it felt like to miss the lunar landing.*

He got upset because *I was* looking at him. *So sorry, I thought you wanted me to watch you kick the ball. I'll just keep moving my eyes and head around erratically so I'm both watching and not watching at any given moment, see if that works for ya.*

He freaked his freak because the sandwich was cut into triangles instead of squares. *Why didn't I realize that triangles are evil? Duhhhh, Bermuda Triangle.*[7]

He went psycho when I wouldn't buy "the fishy movie" for him. It wasn't *Finding Nemo*. It was *JAWS. Silly Mommy, wanting to spare you a lifetime of nightmares and a lifelong fear of fish, boats, beaches, and Richard Dreyfus.*

He had a fit because his shorts were not long enough. *I understand your frustration, but THEY'RE SHORTS!*

And he had a cow because I was singing during what was clearly not song-time. Get with the program, Mommy dumbest. You know, the totally random, arbitrary program that only exists in your child's crazy-ass head.

I know, I know. He's just being a kid. He's doing what kids do. When he's tired or hungry, his whole universe is off its hinges. Even when he's well rested and well fed, he's still a relative newcomer to

---

[7] The Bermuda Triangle is also known as the Devil's Triangle. Legend has it that many ships, airplanes and people's virginities have vanished in this triangular area of the Atlantic.

Earth. Of course he's confused and frustrated and biting my arm hard enough to draw blood because I gave him a spoon instead of a fork—where he comes from they don't use spoons, mom-tard!

He's a good kid who's seeing how the world works, testing the boundaries: *If I freak out about this kernel of corn, will she make that funny sound with her voice and do that silly little dance? God she's adorable. If I go bonkers because she didn't see the ass invader, will she go back so I get to see it one more time? God she's dumb.*

Life is about testing waters and pushing limits and making mistakes. From toddlerville to adulthood, that never, ever ends.

Truth be told, I appreciate his asshole moments. I mean, not while they're happening, but after. When I've wiped away the sweat and I'm ready to reflect on the day. *Damn that was funny when he threw that Brussels sprout at my eye; those baby cabbages pack quite a punch.* These moments are where the hilarity is. That's where I get my stories. In fact, as Max is growing out of pull-ups and inching towards kindergarten, I'm finding myself scant on material.

Some kids, however, never stop generating material, because they're actual assholes. These kids don't just have asshole moments; they have asshole lives. Their assholery is perpetual. Always cranky and/or jerky to other kids and/or total, all-around shit-disturbers. I have seen them. I know some of them. And yes, I want to send them all to a Vietnamese sweat shop. One day, when Max started singing the *Thomas* theme song, messing up a few words as he always does, a friend's little girl yelled, "That's not right! That's *wrong!*" Shut up, ya redundant little twit; my son is having a moment right here and you are fucking shit up. He may have gone on to be the next Tony Bennett, but no, not anymore; he'll just work in the sound room thanks to you, dream-killing ass girl.

There was also this little bastard in Max's soccer squirts league doing everything opposite of the other kids, every goddamn session. Coach said run this way, he'd run the other way. Coach said form a straight line, he'd lie down on the floor where the line should be, messing up the whole system for everybody else. Pretty sure Coach wanted to choke him out with his Scooby-Doo shoelaces. Maybe he had some kind of attention disorder. Whatever. In my books, the A in ADHD stands for asshole.

The worst part of early childhood assholery is when Ma and Pa Asshole don't do anything about Little Anus. "Aw muffin, you know you're not supposed to dropkick the kid with the leg braces. Silly goose." They just laugh at their cute little asshole, or ignore the behaviour altogether, or sit there like Helen Keller at a Megadeth concert and do sweet fuck all. WTF. I mean, it's okay when they've barely got two feet (or cloven hooves) out of the birth canal. Ignoring Max's mischief was quite effective back then. He'd throw his cereal on the floor, I'd ignore it, and he wouldn't bother doing it again. But those were baby tactics. This is serious big boy shit. These little assholes will soon be sprouting upper-lip hair for god's sake. Discipline is key.

I think some parents just don't know how to handle the chaos, so they adopt the attitude of *Kids will be kids, what are ya gonna do?* Here's what you're gonna do, elder ass: you're gonna lay down the law and beat the assholery out of them. Not with your fists, Joan Crawford. With threats! With consequences! Take away everything. Drag him off the soccer field. Post an ad on Kidjiji.[8] If you don't nip it in the bud, it continues, and eventually your whole world becomes a big giant buttocks with your asshole kid spinning around in the middle. Congratulations on raising a full-blown asshole into adulthood with a sense of entitlement but not responsibility, who will go out into the workforce (if he ever leaves your house) expecting 100 grand a year for showing up twenty minutes late every day and photocopying double-sided. One day soon he'll be an asshole parent just like you. Success. Have fun with your asshole grandchildren.

And by the way, disciplining your little assholes doesn't mean you need to be a clamorous bitch. It's actually more maniacal and awesome if you do it calmly, sans emotion: *Game over, ass-tro boy. Get in the car.* One day, Max threatened a little girl at daycare: "If you don't shut up, I'm going to punch you in the face." I was mortified,

---

[8] Like *kijiji*, but instead of selling the toddler bed and kiddy pool, you sell the actual kids.

but split the blame with the Teenage Mutant Ninja Turtles. (You know what teenagers are like.) When we got the news, Andrew and I sat Max down for a chat. We were calm and cool, explaining in the simplest possible terms that we had heard what happened, that hurting other people is just not cool or acceptable, but that everyone makes mistakes and the important thing is to learn from those mistakes and get better. He went into convulsions of guilt and remorse and terror. Hyperventilation ensued. Pretty sure he won't be saying that shit to anyone ever again, except maybe to himself in the mirror. Calm but firm discipline, baby. Freaks 'em right out.

The way I see it: good parents call their kids antichrists, gremlins, jackasses, and jerks. You don't need to call your kid names directly, but if he's being an asshole, make sure he knows it. Make up a word if you have to. How about Shitler?[9] Or how about you keep the sanctimommies off your back and just call him Chucky? To them, it's short and sweet for Charlie. To you, it's your demon child who'll chop you up in little pieces while you sleep. *Stop being such a Chucky. Go get in the car.*

At the very least, call him an asshole to your friends. Or write a book about it that he won't be able to read for at least a few years. Bad mom? You're actually being a good mom by getting the *murder* out of your system before returning to the eye of the shitstorm. With both hands free, instead of locked in a preparatory chokehold, it's so much easier to love the shit out of your little asshole.

[9] The Hitler of asshole children.

What if the hokey pokey
is what it's all about?

— ANONYMOUS

CHAPTER SIX

The Sappy Stuff

So maybe I lied. Maybe I do have some soup.[1]

This chapter is where I get mushy. Because behind my humour is a world of hurt. But no worries, there's still a lot of cursing. Because losing your dad just fuckin' sucks.

The day I found out I was pregnant, my father had a tumor removed from his bowel. Dad died when Max was just nine months old.

It's a hard pill to swallow, knowing my child will never know his grandfather—the person who shaped me more than anyone else on earth. A link in our chain is forever missing and there's not a damn thing I can do about it.

It makes me sad. It makes me crazy. It makes me want to curl up in a ball and die.

But it also makes me want to write—often about pain and loss and death. But hey, as long as I'm writing I'm alive.

---

[1] On page 10 , I said this book was nothing like those chicken soup books. Well, maybe I was wrong. It is one of those books. Sans insufferable cuteness and subsequent gagging.

Growing Things[2]

The usual double-stomp of rubber boots on the front bridge. The whine of the screen door. Then in he burst, bucket in hand, eyes wide with childhood.

He was beseeching us to guess before he was halfway in the house, his first word lost in the flowerbed.

"...how many I got t'day!"

I could hear them knocking around in the salt-beef bucket, like billiard balls rumbling in the belly of a pool table. Potatoes. Maybe seven or eight. Tiny and pitiful and good enough for him.

"Five!"

Five reasons to not wait for anyone's guess.

The scholar emerged from muddy plaid and took his place on the couch, entombed by paperbacks and the first draft of a novel. He took a pen from his pocket, opened his notebook to the back cover, and made five short strokes: four straight-up and one diagonal slashing victoriously through. I could hear it from across the living room.

Ten years ago, I would have rolled my eyes. When other dads were skilled fishermen and farmers, mine was master of the metaphor and *Macbeth*. I was ashamed. Now, I just pretended to be. To treat him the same. To keep things normal.

His thumb was not green but grey with the smudgery of sonnets and sermons. But potatoes were another form of poetry, willed from dead space with living, breathing enthusiasm. His hands were meant to turn pages, not soil, nor fat cod drying on Fogo flakes. At sixteen, he boarded the ferry—to grow his vocabulary, a family, and a scattered stunted spud on a less isolated patch of land.

We were both growing things now. Me, a baby. Him, a tumor. Both feeding off our bodies, getting bigger and stronger and ready to ruin everything. I hurled deals into the great beyond—*take this, let me keep that.* But I kept getting rounder, which I took as a big fat forget-about-it.

---

[2] "Growing Things" won a 2012 Newfoundland and Labrador Arts and Letters Award for Short Fiction. It was far from fiction. Don't tell anyone.

A grapefruit had been growing in Dad's bowel for ten, maybe twenty years. Like a story unfolding while the protagonist's back is turned; he realizes his role midway through the final chapter.

The unluckiest kind of cancer: the one with no symptoms until it has its own postal code. The day they cut it out was the day I saw its replacement—wiggling around on the screen like an upside-down beetle. Three inches of terrible timing.

The size of a new, pink eraser, found on the floor of the high-school hallway, now at home in my sweaty palm. When I was a little girl, Dad would take me with him to fetch a book he had forgotten or make copies of an English quiz on the giant Xerox machine. I'd snoop around the musty staff room and its glorious towers of paper. Steel typewriters were sentinels on every desk, glaring at me with snaggy, metal teeth, warning me to keep my hands to myself. Before we headed home, Dad would find a scribbler and stick it in my pocket. Jackpot. I hoarded them in the bottom drawer of my dresser, rarely making a mark. Blank pages were pressed silk, too easily ruined by an imperfect thought or dangling participle.

Here in my hand now—a photo of my own child. A surge of reality turns it to sandpaper, scratching my fingerprints off until I'm nobody special.

One soul would enter stage left, the other exit stage right. Would they cross paths, brush shoulders, share the space long enough to sprout something forgettable. Or would they pass like dandelion snow on the wind, miss one another by a breath that may as well be a lifetime because, either way, they're strangers. For nine months I waddled around and wondered, trying to believe in miracles, occasionally pondering what would happen to the order of things to come if I threw myself down the stairs.

I remember when these stairs were carpeted orange shag. I'd stomp up to my room, propelling all my teenage angst downward through my body into each stupid step.

"Don't be so opprobrious!"

I drove him to his vocabulary's edge. Once, after I had slammed my bedroom door with tectonic-plate-shifting rage, he came up to my room, took the drawers out of my dresser one by one, and dumped the contents onto the floor, then left without a word. I wrote an apology with fancy glitter pens.

I'm sorry. With a sad face in gold metallic ink.

I was a sad face on a prize pumpkin perched on the edge of his bed when the doctor said the second surgery was a flop. The only hope for a cure, flushed away with my mucus plug. The young surgeon said he still had hope, but I could smell a rotting plum down the hall and the stench of bullshit in his every word. The dead-end news was a rusty trowel in my gut all the way to China. Dad just stared out the window, smiling at the crocuses poking through the patchy March snow.

I lay in a tub of scalding water, silent and numb, a massive earthworm making waves beneath the taut skin of my belly, reminding me I was still alive.

Dad lived in a fortress of paper, bookmarks jutting out to trip those who would disrupt him. I'd approach gingerly, extending a story to be graded. He'd put down his book or journal or pile of essays on *Julius Caesar* and turn to accept my loose leaf, feigning interest in my fat, curly typography. He'd speed-read my meager work, his lips and eyebrows fox-trotting around his face, mesmerized by my genius.

"Well done, daughter!"

He made his mark in just the right spot; never the same thing twice. I'd have another tale for him within the hour. And a sandwich made with every possible ingredient in the fridge, including his own tomatoes grown out back in the greenhouse that used to be the dog pen.

Dad's stitches were closing around his decaying liver, and my eight-pound mass was ready for harvest. But nine days past my due date, I was still holding him in, making time stand still, delaying this and whatever else was about to rock my world. We'd all live off this hope, this little black and white ultrasound picture in my purse. It'd be Christmas Eve forever, the anticipation of good things bringing more joy than their arrival and the sinking knowledge that it'll all soon be over.

By day ten, I was overthrown by the sheer animal urge to bear down. And then there he was, the living, breathing proof that time had passed, things had grown, change was upon us. He was sucking vigorously on the air, searching blindly for my breast. He had just broken my vagina; now he wanted another piece of me. Fast-forward a few months and he'd be laughing hysterically as they lower my father into the ground.

He found his home in the hollow of Poppy's chest where I spent many a morning reading storybooks to the bass drum of his heart. Both their faces: perfect calm. Like they knew something nobody else did. The moment swept me away then dragged me back to earth with a crushing smack of irony: here is the man I will bury, holding the boy who will bury me. Less than an inch of flesh and flannel lay between brand new and irreparably broken. There was a fucked-up beauty in it; I see it now. The meaning of life, colliding in a little blue blanket.

The summer sun let us forget if not heal. Inside, organs were quietly packing it in, ready to call it a life. Outside, we pretended we would all live forever. We danced around the cancer, almost thankful for the bastard because at least we had fair warning. A neighbour had dropped dead with a massive heart attack, lying on the floor in a pool of things left unsaid.

Dad finished his book and grew strawberries, small and pale but sweet. And I grew to love my child, our distraction from the truth, our one perfect thing. Dirty diapers, ceaseless crying, sleepless nights: it was pure joy because it wasn't grief.

By October, the leaves were falling faster and the sands in the hourglass followed suit, swishing by like the beach was finally calling them home. But Dad was slowing down, the pain in his side making it difficult for him to walk. He took his meals on the couch with a dishtowel on his chest for a bib, the checkered cloth enabling a feeble game of peek-a-boo, the boy pulling himself up from the floor to pull away the rag.

"Boo."

Each time, Poppy was still there, to both of our surprise.

I retrieved a notebook from my bottom drawer, unperturbed after all these years. I flipped the pages past my nose. Typewriter ribbons and mildew. The sweet aroma of a simpler time.

The slanted garden sank into a morphine slumber, crab grass

filling in the spaces like it was never there. I collected his poems in a banana box; the colour of the paper whispered the age of each piece— from parched sunflower gold to new lily white.

I christen the little notebook. How do you spell eulogy? That looks right, but not next to the word Dad.

A green, die-cast train comes to a halt at the base of the casket, a boy crawling after it, grunting with glee. Four feet above him his grandfather's hands are folded upon one another. They look odd without a book, or a pen, or a bucket of something plucked from the earth. His face is sunken and clay-like and not his own, but he is surrounded by his favourite things so I know it's him: books, flowers, trees at each corner of his coffin in rich forest green, and people—their faces proud and kind and resilient.

I pick up my boy who chortles at the sight, blissfully oblivious to the colossal shift that has just occurred beneath my feet. There *he* is and here *he* is, the bookends of my existence. The front pocket of my boy's overalls, where a frog should be, is the perfect size for a notebook.

I imagine the casket brimming with tiny potatoes, their gnarly eyes following me around the floral wallpapered room.

Immortal Beloved Words

In the summer of 2012, *Today's Parent* Magazine asked me to write an article about a memorable parenting milestone for their November Johnson's Baby Supplement. Being a writer, I chose to write about Max's first word. But it turned out being about his *second* word, in fact.

The editor de-fucked my story, of course, to make it kosher with the magazine's wholesome brand. My pleasure; anything for a buck a word. The published piece was indeed my story, but it wasn't my voice. So here is my first draft of the article, as I would have had it:

As a writer, I always wondered what my kid's first word would be.

No I didn't. I wondered what he'd look like and prayed that he wouldn't have three testicles, eleven toes, or half a brain.

When Max was born, he was perfect in every way. (Phew.) And he hit his milestones like clockwork: first tooth, first step, and the much-anticipated first word. But instead of the expected "Ma-Ma" or "Da-Da," his first word was "stay." Yes, we have a dog—clearly, a very disobedient one.

Max's first word is not the crux of the story, however. This is actually about his second word: "bye-bye." Pretty typical, right? But the time and place of this sweet "bye-bye" was painfully ironic. We were visiting my hometown, to spend time with my father after the oncologist's final verdict. There was nothing more they could do. *Bye-bye* was something we'd all be saying very soon.

The first time Max said it, we were in my old bedroom, the morning sun peeking through the blinds. I remember waking and looking toward the playpen where he slept. Except he wasn't sleeping; he was standing there, staring at me. When he saw me open my eyes, he shook the side of the playpen with excitement and said, "ba-bye." Not the most appropriate morning greeting, but it was another word in his vocabulary, so I was tickled pink.

Then one afternoon he sniper-crawled across the living room floor and pulled himself up to reach Poppy as he slept. "Ba-bye, ba-bye," he whispered as he patted Dad's face with a chubby hand. Somehow nobody else in the room seemed fazed by this. And he kept doing it. My mom, brother, my parents' friends who often came to visit these days, would all say, "How cute." Maybe they were faking it. Trying to find an ounce of joy in this house of impending doom.

Or maybe nobody else noticed, but I know Dad did. A literature teacher for thirty years, no amount of morphine could shroud the irony. My little boy was unknowinglysaying farewell to the grandfather he'd never remember.

Dad died less than two weeks later at the age of sixty-seven after an eighteen-month battle with cancer. Max was nine months old.

It's okay. Turns out my boy is wise well beyond his years because in his first two words lies the meaning of our entire lives. His second word—*bye-bye*—reminds me that nothing lasts. Not time, youth, beauty, or the human body. And his first word—*stay*—reminds me of the one thing in life that does: words.

Like the book my father finally finished six months before he died. Like the words he last spoke to me five days before the end that now guide my every move. Like the words I write—to Max, about Max—immortalizing our time together, for however long it lasts. And like the words my little boy is learning to form every day. Words he is learning from me that I once learned from my father.

I'll See You in My Dreams

"I guess Max won't know me very well."

I can see Dad now, sitting in the recliner by the window, one leg cocked up over the armrest. He said it like it was no biggie. But attached to that sentence was a heavy weight and it sank my heart to the bottom of the ocean. How sad he was behind the strength. How cheated he felt behind the grace. Funny how I remember the details: the chair, his leg, his sad blinking eyes. I wasn't in my body, but floating above the scene that surely must be a glimpse into someone else's life.

I couldn't believe I was having this conversation; surreal is an understatement. But I was stronger than I knew, and my first instinct was to reassure him that I had a gazillion photos and hours of video footage—of him and Max together. That was all I could muster in that moment. I had no cure, no silver lining, no bullshit optimism. Maybe he was fishing for that, but all I had was the promise of immortality through technology. He seemed satisfied.

Dad was no Carrie Grant, but he loved to be the centre of attention. I had been taping him for months, immortalizing him on a high-def JVC camcorder: quite possibly the best purchase I've ever made. I bought it, not only to record the new little life in our world, but to capture the lives of those who might not be around forever. Which is every one of us, really. I didn't know how things would play out with Dad, but I wasn't taking any chances. Roll tape.

When Dad died, I started showing Max the photos of him right away. At least a couple times a day, I'd ask, "Where's Poppy Jim?"

Max would point to the big, beautiful photo on the wall of two hopeful and childlike faces staring up at the camera from a pillow on the floor.

I put a little photo album on a table in the living room, right in the midst of Mad Max's Thoroughfare. Cover to cover photos of Poppy Jim: mowing the lawn, wearing a silly hat, dancing with a broom, holding the grandson he'd never see grow up.

"That's Poppy Jim!" I'd say with glee, pointing to a pic of the two of them together. "And that's baby Max in his arms!"

I'd poke Max's chubby belly to help him make the connection between the boy in the picture and the boy in the flesh. Sometimes I'd catch him flipping through the album himself, his nimble little digits savagely flipping through the pages. He'd throw it, stomp on it, bend the photos. I didn't care; I had copies. Whatever it took to make Poppy Jim a household name and a familiar face.

It's been over three years now. I still talk about Dad a lot. I tell

Max stories about crazy Poppy Jim. Max thinks it's a riot. But I've relaxed about it now. It's okay if we don't think or talk about Dad all the time. Some days I don't think about him much at all. Maybe that's because I don't need to. My life is full and happy, even without him here, in part because he *was* here. I'm okay without him, because he helped make it so. I don't think about him all the time, but I have thirty-plus years of him squirreled away for the winter.

He does cross my mind at one particular time every day: when I'm tucking Max into bed. We read a storybook, turn out the light, and say, "Goodnight, Poppy Jim up in the sky." After this sign-off, Max likes to remind me, quite matter-of-factly: "Yeah, Poppy Jim died. He is killed." And, without fail, he goes on to mention that Spook and Lacey—my husband's childhood pooches—are also dead. "They is killed too." To him, there's no difference. Dead dad, dead dog, dead mouse, dead spider. In some ways he is exactly right. Death is a fly in a web, a crisp leaf in your hand, and a father in a casket. Everything goes to sleep, eventually. There's no getting out alive.

Bedtime seems like a good time to remind Max of Dad, with the former going to sleep and the latter enjoying a dirt nap like it's nobody's business. As you know, I'm not much of a believer. Dad dying when Max was just nine months old was not part of some great divine plan. It did not happen for a reason. It happened because our bodies are full of cells and sometimes abnormal ones grow uncontrollably and they don't give a sweet shit about the terrible fuckin' timing.

But sometimes when Max drifts off to sleep after our usual cuddle, I like to think another comforting arm takes the place of mine. I imagine the two of them together, enjoying an ice cream cone somewhere on the outskirts of Dreamland, right where the clouds end and the Great Beyond begins. No talking, just licking. Licking and smiling and knowing. "You're Poppy Jim," Max says with his eyes. "And you're Pop's boy," Dad winks. "And ice cream is a wonderful thing." They both nod in agreement. And they're not strangers anymore.

Father, Son, and Holy Shit

If we value honesty so much, why do we tell our kids there's a Santa Claus? One of the most elaborate lies of all time. But I guess this opens up a whole can of worms that reek of bullshit. Santa. The tooth fairy. The Easter bunny. Heaven. God. Oh stop your gasping. There are over 2,500 recorded "gods"—what makes yours the right one? Because you spell it with a capital G?

Just short of a year after our shittiest day, my brother and I went back to the homestead to attend a memorial service hosted by the local funeral home. A tribute to all those who had died in the past twelve months, our father included. Hymns were sung. Holy words were spoken. I heard the word "father" over and over and over. But they were not talking about my father. They were talking about *the* father. You know, the one with the Son and Holy Spirit to boot. That elusive, threefold enigma. Righteous dudes, who is this "god" person we're talking about? I'm here to think about *my* father, not the father of humanity who seems more the stuff of legends than reality. I know my dad existed, and still exists in me and in everything I do, but you have to admit—the rest sounds a little sketchy.

When we sang "How Great Thou Art," I was singing about Dad. How great *he* was.

> When through the woods and forest glades I wander,
> I hear the birds sing sweetly in the trees;
> when I look down from lofty mountain grandeur
> and hear the brook and feel the gentle breeze…

My dad loved nature. So for me, those lyrics are about what he enjoyed, not what "god" created.

Don't get me wrong; I was touched by the event. The mutual loss. A room full of people who would celebrate (or lament) that coming Christmas with an empty chair at the dinner table. Words floated up into the air above our sadness, spelling out *I know how you feel.*

I could feel the genuine sympathy of those employed by the Grim Reaper himself, working under a cloud of death, day in and day out: a well-deserved paycheck. In the past fifty-two weeks, eighty-two people had died in our town and the surrounding area.

That's about one and a half deaths a week. And with an ever-aging community, those numbers will continue to rise. Corpses flying. Death is big business. In fact, another funeral home recently opened. Maybe the cost of caskets will drop. Deadly.

I giggled a couple of times. A few righteous brothers were raising their hands to the sky, eyes closed, all full of the trinity and such. Dad would have looked at me with that notoriously foolish face, subtly mocking the drama, so I did the same to Mom. When one musical act was performing, a hot mess indeed, I drew a thumbs-down sketch on my program and flashed it at Mom. When I saw her blank-faced expression, I took a second glance at my drawing and realized it looked just like a penis.

How do you take the whole god thing seriously when your brain is full of dinosaurs and evolution and comparative anatomy? We came from fish, you know. Explain that, Pope. And yes, I know there are wonders all around us that seem to defy science and logical explanation. But all in all, the god thing is a bit of a stretch. I mean, what kind of all-powerful being would allow the Holocaust to happen, and my third-grade mullet? I guess I'm atheist, but for my god-fearing mother's sake let's call me a half-assed believer. Even though I'm a firm believer that if you're going to do anything, you should do it with your whole ass.

But even though I think it's poppycock, I'm going to tell Max about Jesus.

See, we are of that new order of families whose Sunday routine consists of lazing around in our jammies, eating cereal, and watching movies about space travel. "Church" is just a picture in Max's *Little People* book.

Recently, while visiting my mom at the homestead for Easter, Max came downstairs exclaiming, "Jesus was back alive!" After fighting the urge to tell him that Jesus was a zombie who slowly morphed into a bunny, my straight-up bedtime story had stuck. "Jesus died," he recollected. "But when it became Easter day, he came alive again." Mom was thrilled. My atom-splitting science teacher of a husband, however, just glared at me, his thick eyebrows twisting into tornadoes. *What have you been teaching our son?* "Don't worry, honey," I assured him, "I'm not getting all Jesusy on ya."

I went to church on Easter Sunday with my mom and Max. One time too many, I suppose, for an outspoken skeptic or atheist or agnostic or whatever the hell I am. People were moving away from me in church to avoid the projectile splinters that would surely result from a pew-splitting bolt of lightning.

I was raised in the church. My father was an Anglican lay minister for fifty years. I sang in the choir for ten. I know all the words to several hymns. I even have a favourite—"The King of Love, My Shepherd Is." It still gives me chills. Possibly because I imagine the "shepherd" is Channing Tatum in a loincloth, but I digress. Now, do I think it's all a bunch of biblical bunk? Pretty much. I just can't bring myself to go to church anymore; it's all so silly. And I can't seem to shake the fact that some of the world's most gifted minds thought so too. Charles Darwin. Albert Einstein. Helen Keller. Ernest Hemingway. John Lennon. Jodie Foster.

But I'm not one of those hypocrites who expects to get married and buried in the church but never steps foot inside in-between. We got hitched by the mayor, and let it be known: when I go tits-up, you can throw my ashes into the cavity of an old, broken typewriter.

But I haven't completely forsaken church. I can appreciate the sense of community, and I guess I'm still open to the possibilities. Refusing to go—never ever—would be like declaring I know something for certain, and that is neither true nor possible. The burden of proof is with you though, Jesus lovers. So forgive me for skipping church and watching *E.T.* with my family instead. I may not be wrapped in the arms of Jesus, but I'm wrapped in somebody's arms and somebody's wrapped in mine. This is what's real to me. This is my heaven. Send me a Jesus memo when you find something.

But even though I'm not all Jesusy, it doesn't mean Max can't be. So I took him to church on Easter morning. As his mother, it's on me to teach him how to be polite and share and wipe his arse, but it's not my job to tell him what to believe. Especially when I don't have the slightest clue myself. It's my job to guide him, and show him some of the options—like the story of Jesus and Easter and Christmas and Satan—and then he can decide for himself.

Besides, I reckon there are worse things to be than Jesusy. As far as I know, Jesus was a kind, gentle, compassionate man who lived humbly and judged no one. If more so-called Christians acted more like that, maybe I wouldn't have such distaste for the whole thing.

Anyway, even though I'm not much of a believer myself, I tell my son about Jesus. So that one day, when he realizes it's all a bunch of hogwash, it won't be "because Mom told me so." It'll be "because that is what I think." On the other hand, if he decides it's all true, I am open to be enlightened.

Would my dad roll over in his grave if he heard my cynical discourse? Probably. But he's the one who taught me to use my head and speak my mind. So really—it's all his fault.

First Born: The Furkid Gets the Shaft

There's a hill in our backyard that makes for the perfect tobogganing experience. Sometimes at night, we hear the laughter of children enjoying the snow-covered knoll, not realizing it's on our property or maybe not caring. No odds, because we don't care either—whoop it up, kids! But next time, pick up your chip bags, ya little bastards.

At twenty months, Max had his first day on the slopes of Chez Murphy. The whole family had fun, but none more than our three-year-old. You know, the kid with the tail and the beard.

We started to deck out in boots, hats, and mittens. Splash, our Portuguese water dog, knew what this meant: the great outdoors was near. She's no dummy; she's been fetching beer from the fridge since she was five months old. Don't believe me? It's on YouTube, bitches.

Dogs smile with their tails, and her fluffy appendage was grinning from fuzzy butt cheek to fuzzy butt cheek. Andrew has only to say, "Where's my fun pants?" (that's code for snow pants), and Splash starts to lose her furry little mind, growling eagerly and encircling him with her leash in her mouth.

Andrew and Max were the first to test the speed of our new foam sled. They flew down the hill with Splash racing along beside them, occasionally heaving her four-pawed self toward the sled to derail them.

When it was my turn to slide down with the boy, Splash stayed at the top of the hill with Andrew. But when Max and I came to a stop at the bottom and looked up, Splash was racing toward us full-tilt, tongue flapping in the sun-kissed winter wind. Half a second before she got to us, she veered to her left, avoiding us by a hair. After the exhilaration of the descent, El Mutto's antics supplied an unexpected final rush. Well, not really that unexpected. That's so her. So full of life. A reminder that life is nothing if not fun.

Max, in all his childlike wonder, has shown me the meaning of life. I remember when we'd take him out of the car and the first thing he'd look for was the moon.

"Mooooon?" he'd say, like an uncertain cow, pointing toward the radiant orb in the sky.

The light of the moon. The crunch of snow underfoot. The taste of fresh pineapple. He's discovering the simple joys of being alive. And I get to watch.

But he's not the first one to show me these simple joys. Splash was my first teacher of this lesson of lessons. (Well my 'rents were the first, really. But Splash came along when I needed a cosmic reminder.) In a world that feels more like a race than a journey, with people accumulating more and more and feeling less and less, Splash's humble requirements keep me grounded. A walk, a rub, and a cookie. A dog's life: how intrinsically simple it is. As I type this, she's lying next to me on a couch big enough for eight of us, secretly hoping for a scratch or a treat, but content to just be here, with me. Quiet companions. I type, and she snores, occasionally raising her head from my thigh when she hears a car go by—could it be *him*? When I turn off the television and the lights, she'll know—it's time for one last tinkle in the garden and then bedtime. Sometimes when she's tired, she heads for the bedroom, stops halfway, and looks back as if to say, "You comin' or what, missus?"

Since Max came along, Splash has inevitably taken the backseat—literally. She used to ride shotgun. At red lights, people in nearby cars would point at us and laugh, realizing the proud passenger was a dog and not a person. Now she's confined to the backseat, partly because the front seat is full of baby crap and partly because she chooses to be back there with Max and his delectable food-covered face.

She doesn't get the exercise she used to or deserves, but we're trying, and when Max gets a little bigger and less insane in the membrane, we'll take more outings together—all four of us. Good times are ahead. Like any dog's life, hers will be too short. In fact, we recently learned that Splash's father, Kingsley, died at the young age of seven. Colon cancer. Something else Splash and I have in common. We owe this bitch. It's our duty to make these ten to fifteen years as rich as possible. She doesn't ask for much. If only the people next door felt a fraction of that sense of responsibility. On that first day on the home slopes, as Splash frolicked freely in the backyard, their dog watched longingly from his six-foot leash, as always. Just another lawn ornament, begging to be stolen.

One thing is for sure—there is no shortage of love here. She sleeps with us every night. (Yes, Dog Whisperer, I know that's unwise, but bite me.) We wake up in the morning and turn to see sleeping Splash, four perfectly straight paws pointing skyward. Without my glasses on, I see a furry, upside-down table. I'm no morning person, but how can I be cranky when I wake up to such a ridiculously cute sight?

If you're petless, you probably don't understand. But I won't count you out. My dad didn't have a dog, not since I was a toddler (R.I.P. Skip), but he loved all creatures. I think Dad saw the purity in those big, brown, fur-trimmed eyes. More than once I caught him slipping her treats. A few summers ago, we were all at my brother's for dinner. Splash was tied to the back deck, staring at the windows and doors, whining to come inside where the people (and the food!) were abound. We just ignored her; we'd be going home soon. But a couple of times, I caught a glimpse of Dad through the window, kneeling down to give her a gentle pat on the head or a drink of cool water. He recognized her. He saw her for what she was: the purest soul on the property and, ironically, the only one not allowed in the house.

Rain, Drizzle, Fog, and Family

Newfoundland and Labrador's climate is classified as "humid continental," better known as "shit storm." We receive less than 1,600 hours of sunshine per year, much lower than the Canadian average of 1,925 hours. Fuck you, Canada.

The provincial capital, St. John's, is nicknamed Fog City. Our fog is infamous. Founded in 1497, we are North America's oldest city, but it's a miracle anyone discovered us at all. The fog is often accompanied by strong onshore winds. And, while winds usually disperse fog, here the fog is too widespread for this to occur. Fog sakes.

One day a couple Augusts ago, the day's high temperature was eleven degrees. I woke up to the usual rain, drizzle, and pea-soup fog with doughboy clouds congealed into a grey pastry, kiboshing any trace of the elusive yellow orb, the name of which I can't quite remember, like a distant cousin you see at weddings but never talk to. It was being called Augember. Fogust. Blahgust. However you say it, the summer of 2011 here on the east coast of Newfoundland was a real kick in the pants.

And speaking of pants, when would we ever get to take them off? That summer, like most, my shorts just sat there in the drawer, sad and lonely and wishing they were longer. No odds; I can't even see what I'm wearing from the neck down. The fog is so thick, I could be wearing snowshoes and a strap-on for all I know.

But hey, we're hardy Newfoundlanders. We're mothers! We thrust humans out of our vaginas, for Christ's sake! Surely a little bit of RDF can't break us. But why oh why must we go on and on about it? Why oh why am I going on about it right now? It's a disease, I tell you, a *disease*!

In June of 2011, Newfoundland received the most consecutive days of rain in the province's history. But it was the people gushing about the rain that dragged me down like a wet mitt. How I didn't karate chop someone every hour is amazing to me. When July finally arrived with some sun, I thanked the high heavens. People would shut their umbrellas, and their gobs.

Hey, everyone everywhere talks about the weather. Right now, there are little green men on distant planets saying, "Another meteor shower coming today, fellas. Put up the windows on the SuperSaucer and activate the dry-fit force field." But in Martian. Or Jupiterian. Or Uranish. Whatever.

But I challenge anywhere in the galaxy to compete with our obsession with the weather. Here in Newfoundland, it's a non-stop, year-round conversation. Geographically inspired, I suppose: we are a pointy appendage of the earth jutting out into the North Atlantic like an index finger flipping Africa the bird. We're just bitter because when this chunk of rock broke off from Africa during continental drift, we left the tropical climate behind. And the zebras. Raw deal.

Our weather defines us. When we get twenty feet of snow, it makes the news. When we get a green Christmas, everyone complains that it's just not "Christmassy" without the white stuff and *that* makes the news. I pray for armed robberies and hijackings just so there's something else for CBC News to report! When it rains or hails or blows a gale, the chatter ensues. And when it's warm, well hold onto your sweaty shorts, it's the first thing to fall from our lips: "Some hot t'day, missus! Garge, turn on the fan, I'm just about gone."[3]

Let's face it: we are not clinging to these shores for the weather. It's putrid with the exception of four to six sunny weeks of the year, during which time you must nonetheless pack a wool sweater just in case the wind blows "nar'wes," as grandfather would say. (If you're a snow-savourin' winter person, go shine your snowmobile with your EI check; this rant is not for you.)

We talk about the RDF with a scowl every day of our windswept lives, and yet we stay here, hanging on for dear life as the wind yanks our flowers out of their pots and our fathers out of their boats. We cling like moss to a rock as snow beats down our fences, bends our shovels, and breaks our backs. We hang on, waiting for the blink of summer to arrive with a couple gallons of blueberries, a few fresh cod, a half-dozen visits to the beach, and one-fifth of a tan. Then batten down the hatches, it's mid-September and summer is a distant memory. (If you're a leaf-loving autumn person, go knit a scarf; this

---

[3] Translation: It's so hot today, girlfren'. George, turn on the fan before I start to melt.

verbiage is for someone else.) We're a bunch of cling-ons.

And since we're not going anywhere, we really should stop complaining about the weather. Shut up or ship out. Maybe all you winter and autumn-lovin' peeps got it right after all: love it or leave it. Good for you (freaks).

Why do we stay here? Family, mostly. But it's something else too. Pride? Maybe. But it's more than that. It's a sense of belonging, which you become acutely aware of when you leave. I went to university just across the gulf in Halifax, and as much as I loved that vibrant city, I was a foreigner in a foreign land. Do all displaced people feel this way? Maybe, but on a lesser scale, I reckon. Perhaps it's the innate uniqueness of the Newfoundlander that makes the creature stand out from the crowd; a species of strange dialect and foolish disposition that can make blending in—an important feat for the paranoid, unsure, and immature almost-adult— virtually impossible.

The city of Halifax looked me square in the face and asked, "Who the hell are you and what are you doing here?" Frustrated and lost, I stared back and shouted, "Where's the chips, dressing, and gravy, beyotch?" (Sadly, CD&G does not exist beyond this island.)

Here, my homeland asks me no questions and I tell it no lies. I am at ease. This is the weather-ravaged soil from which I came, and to which I shall return. I don't quite fit anywhere else. And I certainly don't *sound* right anywhere else. I present ad campaigns via telephone to clients on the mainland. I'm pretty sure they think I'm a nine-year-old leprechaun girl.

So naturally I am happy to grow my son here, planted in home soil like rhubarb. Robust and resilient with the makings of an awesomely delicious jam.

I have family and friends raising their youngsters on the mainland with only a sense of Newfoundland patriotism that their parents instill in them. I want to pity them for raising mainlanders instead of true Newfoundlanders, but perhaps they're lucky in a whole other way. They get a taste of the magic when they come to visit Nan and Pop in the summer and probably appreciate tenfold that which we often take for granted.

Despite the stomach-turning weather and the transplanted loved ones in foreign soil, I am lucky to be able to make a go of it here. I am raising my boy like a proud Newfoundland flag. Minus the pole. Well, not really. There's a pole. That's gross.

He watches the tractor in the field behind the house roll hay into big, fat marshmallows. "Big tractor," he points and shouts. Every tractor and truck is big, even the little ones. He chases Nanny and Poppy Murphy on the trails of Mount Pearl, charming passers-by with his Irish looks and dropped Hs. Soon, he'll play 'ockey in the cow-path streets of Torbay and fish side-by-side with his daddy at the pond just up the road. You know, when Turbo Ginger learns to reel in more than trouble. He'll catch pricklies in a bucket down by the landwash in Badger's Quay, then stab them to death with a pointy stick. *Excellent maiming, son!* He'll collect flat stones on Cape Freels beach where Nanny Shirley—my mom—once hosted tea parties. *Would you like some sand in your tea, madame? Why yes, yes I would.* He'll go squishing toward Nanny's house in his mucky rubber boots when his little stomach starts to rumble for a feed of cod tongues (I'll tell him it's chicken) and buttered homemade bread. *Now take off dem boots on the bridge, ya little rascal. I just cleaned the floor!* He'll go to Fogo Island and stand on the very spot where Poppy Jim was born, and write his first bad poem about the sea that I'll immortalize in a scrapbook. And yes, half the time he'll be wearing a sweater to ward off the biting nar'wes wind.

Rain. Drizzle. Fog. It's wind at our backs, thrusting us forward. It's cold in our bones, huddling us together for warmth, binding us forever. It's time to relish the RDF. And be glad it's not relish falling on our heads, perhaps. It's time to find joy in this motherfuckin' stuff. Ahem. Presenting…The Benefits of Our Bloody Hellish Weather:

1. It saves us money on Speedos. My husband just has the one. It's white. So is he. Very white. So when he's in it, it disappears. Then he asks me to play Find-the-Baloney. Stick with Pictionary.
2. It saves us money on summer recreation. Who needs pony rides and water parks? Sitting around the house in my fat pants

eating Kraft Dinner straight from the pot literally costs me nothing. Less the cost of the KD and my self-esteem.

3. It saves our creamy white skin from dangerous UV rays. Sure, the void of life-giving Vitamin D can spiral us into deep depression, but at least we'll have wrinkle-free skin all around that perma-frown.

4. It deters us from swimming and boating, and therefore decreases our chances of drowning. High five, survivor! It also makes death by humpback very unlikely.

5. It keeps me away from the beaches. Yay—no sand in my cracks. And no need to put the toothbrush anywhere but in my mouth.

6. It saves us money on propane. Only a carnivorous tree frog would barbecue in this rain. And with all this fog, we can't even see the grill anyways. We could be eating hooves and bungholes for all we know. Oh wait…hot dogs. We are eating hooves and bungholes. Never mind.

7. Puddles. It's why god created rubber boots. And rubber ducks. And pedestrians who walk too close to the curb.

8. It's too wet and windy to put clothes on the line, so into the dryer they go. I know, there's nothing like the smell of clothes fresh off the clothesline. But I can do without the spiders and the crispy jeans. I know the electric dryer is a waste of energy. (Sorry, Ed Begley Jr.) But it does save *my* energy! I have better things to do with my time, like coming up with this list. If it can save one life, all that fabric softener will be worth it.

Escape from the Hood

One of the greatest gifts a mother can give her child is to abandon him or her once in a while. Seriously. We get so consumed by the demands on us to be everything to everyone, we start to resent it. All of it. And all of *them*: the big boss at work and the little boss at home. Suddenly it's their fault you just drove for an hour on the highway in the wrong direction before realizing it. (Yes, this

happened.) Suddenly it's their fault your purse is a shit abyss from which you lost a key to an apartment where you were staying while out of town on a TV shoot which you had to pay $175 to replace. (This happened too, FML.)

The only solution is getting out. Not forever, deadbeat, but for a while. A couple of weeks, a couple of days, a couple of hours. Take what you can get, sister. Recharge the ol' mommy batteries before you resort to battery. You know what they say: absence makes the heart grow less murderous. It's like when the husband goes out on the town. He is always extra affectionate the following day. Because he got away from us for the night, blew off some steam, and realized how lucky he is to have a hot piece of ass for a wife waiting for him at home. Or maybe he just feels guilty about screwing that dirty pirate hooker in the bathroom stall. Whatever. Likewise, when I get away for a while, I return with renewed appreciation for peeps (and without gonorrhea).

One of my first escapes from the Hood was to Florida with my colleague and gal pal, Kim Power. (Everyone calls her Kim Power, not just Kim. I'm not sure why.) Max was approaching two and all kinds of crazy. I had to get away. But it was much harder to escape the Hood than I realized. The entrapment started before I even left.

I had those thoughts—you know the ones—as I was leaving the house at 4:30 a.m. to catch my flight. I peeked in at my little copper-haired prince in sweet slumber, gently stroked the curls that adorned his perfect forehead, and squeezed one last splurge of love from his meaty little arm before I headed for the door. He crossed my mind again when I was 30,000 feet in the air, looking down at the sea of clouds. You know the feeling. That little surge of dread: *What if I never see him again?* Hey, it happens.

Things got off to a rocky start. (I said you needed to get away. I didn't say it was going to be paradise.) I got apprehended at Customs for having an apple in my knapsack. *A Canadian apple? That's it, bend over, we need to do a cavity search for illegal fruits and vegetables.* I'm surprised they didn't make me wear the scarlet letter: A for apple tart. They led me away to a special room and proceeded to interrogate me. "What else are you hiding in your luggage, ma'am?" They were so mean. I wished I had packed a duck suit, a small pumpkin, and a butt plug. Just to see their faces. I heard the heavy door opening and looked to see Kim Power being escorted in; she had a bejezus apple in her bag too.

We safely arrived on the ground in Florida, but the Hood was haunting me still. There were storks everywhere! You know, the birds that bring the babies. A constant reminder that there really should be an easier way to reproduce. And were they trying to tell me something? If I wasn't doubling up on the BCPs, I'd have been peeing on a stick every hour. Or beating Andrew with a bigger stick. Fertile bastard.

The driving was no walk in the park, either. We had a sweet rental. But our GPS was clearly on the Rape-Me setting. Instead of keeping us on major roadways, it zigzagged us through the darkest and shadiest areas of St. Petersburg. Kim Power kept re-locking the doors to keep the crazies out. I felt like we were on an episode of *Cops: The Stupid Newfie Special.* But no worries—St. Pete is the old-rich-white-guy capital of Florida. Daytona Beach is actually the state's rape capital.

And as if things couldn't get any wackier, on one of the last days of our trip, I got stung on the thumb by a bee. I was actually pirouetting through the parking lot of our company condo and I whacked a bee on the bum with my thumb. Ouch. Right in the hitchhiker. Who gets stung on the thumb by a bee? Seriously. Maybe it was time to go home.

See, that's the thing. Imperfection is the key. Sure, I enjoyed a week of sun, seafood, shopping, and lesbian beach orgies (Kim Power's idea), but it wasn't flawless: wicked apple, near rape, kamikaze bee, etc. These bumps in the exotic road serve as a reminder that the world beyond the Hood is not perfect either.

From a distance, away from the snarl of the daily routine, we see more clearly the life we left behind and the people we were trying to escape. Missing their faces, imagining life without the loveable friggers, we realize our mission was always doomed to fail. There is no escaping your own heart.

Rockabye baby, in the treetop.
Don't you know a treetop
is no safe place to rock.

— SHEL SILVERSTEIN, "ROCKABYE"

CHAPTER SEVEN

Just Another Manic Mommy

Having a baby is an incredibly lonely time. Yes, there is immeasurable joy. But mixed in with that joy is a generous helping of inexplicable solitude.

It's probably not that hard to explain, actually. I'm home alone. My husband is at work. The dog is dangling her head and paws from the edge of the couch, sighing loudly every hour or so, wishing she had opposable thumbs so she could pop the cap off the aspirin and ascend to Rainbow Bridge.[1] All my friends are at work, talking and laughing and achieving. I'm at home in a dirty t-shirt that gathers around my gunt, with a baby in my arms who can't even smile yet. I am watching reruns of *Road to Avonlea* and feeling a little too akin to the Clydesdales in Alec King's stable. Better to watch *Avonlea* than the news though, where everything is death and tragedy and rolling heads. I haven't even showered yet and it's four in the afternoon. And, according to my handy dandy day planner, I will be doing this again tomorrow and the day after that.

---

[1] Rainbow Bridge is where pets go when they die. Especially gay poodles.

I'm sitting in the glider with nothing but my thoughts. Oh, and the baby. I'm feeding him from my bovine teats for the seventeenth time today, bloody snacker. I'm looking around the room, hating the hideous paint choice, wondering what year it is, and thinking. Pondering. Asking. Why didn't anyone tell me motherhood would feel like this? Why is there so much injustice in the world? Why? Why, goddamn it, why?

Danger, disease, hypocrisy, religious fanaticism, intolerance, injustice, superficiality, and crime. All kinds of atrocities come to mind when there's a creature feasting on your fun bags and you have nothing to do but surrender.

This is *your* creature. Your creation. Your bear cub. The only thing you have left to live for. And you just want to stuff him right back inside your mangled meat curtains to spare him the horrors of the world.

When the Bow Breaks

Remember baby walkers? The ancestor of the exersaucer with wheels on the bottom? I don't remember them, but I have photos of my miniature self in one, rolling around the house at breakneck speed with a cookie in one hand and a death wish in the other. These contraptions led to many injuries, and yet they were a household staple for nearly a hundred years.

In 2004, Canada had finally seen enough baby-sized chalk outlines and became the first country to ban the sale, importation, and advertisement of baby walkers. It was either that or ban stairs, and that was a little ridiculous. Even selling second-hand baby walkers at yard sales and flea markets is illegal. Take note: if you're harbouring a baby walker in your home, you could be fined up to $100,000 or sentenced to up to six months in jail. You'd get a more lenient punishment for making toddler pie.

Even without those munchkin mutilators, it's still a dangerous world out there. And by out there I mean in here—in our house. It's just a bungalow with a couch, a TV, a fridge, a samurai sword collection—the usual stuff. But a toddler can find trouble in a room full of cotton and rainbows. Especially when he's half chimpanzee. In Max's first year and a half of life, he fell down the stairs. He tumbled face-first out of his highchair, twice. He busted his lip at least a half dozen times. Once, he even bit his tongue so bad, I thought he had bitten it clean off and swallowed it.

I still remember the horror of that morning. I was in bed (my turn to catch a few extra Zs) when I was jolted awake by Max's blood-curdling screams. As Andrew reached my bedroom door with the wailing boy in his arms, I was mortified by the sheer amount of blood. His sleepers were saturated. It was like baby Hannibal Lecter had just eaten his first liver. He had, in fact, fallen down and chomped a huge gash in his tongue: one of the pitfalls of having fourteen teeth at ten months of age. Amazingly, his tongue healed in a day or two. It is one of the fastest healing organs in the human body. Who knew?

Max has not swung from the chandeliers or rafters, but only because we don't have chandeliers or rafters. He works with what he's got—cupboards and drawers and daggers. Once, when I was washing the dishes, he was playing near my leg, pulling dishrags from the drawer. I noticed a sudden silence—silence is the toddler alarm bell—and I looked down to see Max standing there, peering up at me with wonder, with a giant meat cleaver in his hand. Holy shit, Jack the Ripper Junior! I calmly removed the mini machete from his hand and breathed a sigh of relief. So that's where I put that sucker.

All this and not a single trip to the emergency room. Yet.[2]

Safety. It's a tricky thing. Obviously, I try to be cautious, but I don't want to be one of those mothers who follows her kid's every move, gasping every time he stumbles. I use common sense, but I don't overdo it. If I refused him everything, I'd be uttering one, long, drawn-out *nooooo* all day, every day. The way I see it, a scattered bump, bruise, or pinch is a good thing. A lesson in cause and effect. If he puts both hands in the wood-chipper, for example, he'll only do it once.

---

[2] Clearly I wrote this before the treadmill incident of Christmas 2011.

But hey, we don't tempt fate. The meds and chemicals are safely stored away up high. We pay attention to product recalls, kinda sorta. We don't leave him unattended in the bathtub; if we can't give him our full attention, we just don't bathe him. We cut up his sugar so he doesn't choke. If the wire is frayed, we stop him from chewing on it. We don't let him run with scissors, only staplers, tape dispensers, pencils, stuff like that. And we don't keep the knives under the dishrags anymore. Now we just keep them in plain sight on the countertop next to the matches.

Put down the phone; I'm exaggerating. But the truth is, no matter how many precautions we take, kids hurt themselves from time to time. Their curiosity and sense of adventure, compounded by the fact that they're just learning how to use their bodies, make it inevitable. Since we can't prevent every nick and bruise, we should be prepared. Stock up the first aid kit, become a CPR ninja, and always be ready to hug it out. Because when the world sucks (or bites, cuts, or scratches), what they need even more than a band-aid is to know everything's going to be alright. Mommy's here.

Crappy Easter from the Party Pooper

When did Easter become a second Christmas? Seriously, when did this happen? Was it always this way and I've just been living under a rock at the entrance to the tomb of Jesus? Now that I have my own egg-seeking chocolate muncher, other moms are asking, "So what are you giving Max for Easter?"

"Uhhh…I gave him life, so I guess I'll just continue letting him live?"

"Oh." (Read: you terrible mother.)

"Why? Am I supposed to give him gifts for Easter?"

"Well, you don't have to. But, you know, some parents," she means *good* parents, "give their kids candy eggs, chocolate bunnies…"

"Oh yeah, I could do that. They sell that stuff at the liquor store, right?"

"…and clothes, toys, bikes, video games…"

"Shit, son! The Easter Bunny is trying to outdo Santa. Is this revenge for the fur-trimmed suit?"

Call Social Services or the Grinch Police because Max ain't gettin' none of it. Okay, maybe he'll get one chocolate bunny, but that's it. That's enough. He's a toddler. A chocolate bunny is bigger than his head! Well, not really; he has an enormous head. But you get my point. And between the loot of Christmas and his birthday, he's got more clothes than the combined wardrobes of Suri Cruise and the Housewives of Orange County.

Christmas is bad enough. Commercialized up the ass. What's that? The baby Jesus was born? Excellent. I think I'll go drop a grand at Toys R Us to celebrate. Yay, Jesus. I mean I guess I get it: Christmas is about love, and we show our love by giving each other frivolous junk. Makes sense. And at least it's just once a year, right? Once a year ain't so bad. It's not like we're stuck paying off the debt for months afterwards. That never happens.

But wait. Just a couple of months later, here comes the big ol' floppy-eared fuck-tard with his bountiful basket of bunk. As you know by now, I'm not much of a believer, but even I know Easter is supposed to be about the ultimate sacrifice and resurrection of Jesus. On Good Friday, there was no big-ass bunny hanging on the cross with rusty nails in his paws and blood trickling down his fluffy white fur. And when they rolled away the stone of the tomb, they didn't find a stockpile of Cadbury Creme eggs in there (although it does sound bloody delicious). We've totally crucified Easter over the last couple millennia.

Thirty years ago, when I was a little chick, it was so wonderfully simple. Birds tweeting. Lilies blooming. A feed of turkey or turrs after church. A handful of little chocolate eggs wrapped in colourful foil hidden around the living room. (We'd find one sneaky bugger months later and wonder if it was still good to eat.) And a chocolate bunny that I'd methodically consume, bit by bit, over the next week. Ears first, ass last.

But look at it now: we've gone and complicated the hell out of it. We've got our kids thinking every time there's a Jesus event—Christmas, Easter—they get a barrel of bling. And then we post photos of it on Facebook—you know, so the kids in Africa can see how much we love Jesus. Jesus doesn't equal love, silly rabbit. Jesus equals candy and chocolate and new clothes and pastel-coloured shit and a week of no school. In fact, we've probably got our kids loving the whole crucifixion thing a little too much: *Hurry up and nail that dude to the cross already so I can get my sugar rush on.*

Nice trick, Bible boinkers. I imagine, deep inside the bowels of the Vatican, there's a candy factory where they lace little fudge bunnies with extra sugar to fuel the addiction of the world's kids to the sweet story of Easter. And it's not just the Catholics. I'm sure the Archbishop of Cadbury is in on it too.

If we're going to give our kids gifts for Easter, at least we could tell them *why*. You know, as a symbol of the ultimate gift of Christ or something. But sadly, some of us are just not that bright. Or maybe we just can't bring ourselves to tell our kids about the Lamb of God because it sounds an awful lot like the shit of sheep. So we tell them a mascot-sized bunny brought the goods. Because that sounds so much better.

Here's an idea. If we insist on showering our kids with Easter shat, how about we throw in a few t-shirts? Give our kids oodles of candy, toys, and gadgets, and make them wear one of these shirts to give credit where credit is (supposedly) due:

"Thank u 4 the iPod, G-ziz."

"Jesus gave me salvation…and Smarties!"

"Jesus died for my sins…and this scooter."

"These Lego were made possible by the very generous contributions of zombie Jesus."

We should make our kids wear these t-shirts when they get their picture taken with the Easter bunny at the mall. Just a couple months ago, we forced the poor little fools to sit on the lap of a creepy old man in a velvet suit and ratty beard. Now it's time to get cozy with some sweaty guy in an enormous rabbit suit. And seriously, have you seen an Easter bunny that's not fuckin' scary as shit? Every time I stumble upon Max's copy of *The Velveteen Rabbit*, I shudder.

So what other bullshit Christian holidays shall we commercialize to death? We have this dry period around summer with no excuse to further spoil our already rotten children. How about we have a Noah's Ark Day and give our kids expensive watercraft? Every child needs a Sea-Doo. Or wait, maybe we could call it Jonah and the Whale Day. That way, we could have some dude dress up as a humpback and make our kids sit in his mouth.

Friendship Is Hard

About once a year, I reunite with my childhood friends. Between the six of us, we have thirteen kids (so far). Where has the time gone? How did this happen? Yes, yes, penises, I know.

We used to be everything to each other. Swapping clothes before the dance, smoking cigarettes behind the community hall, hiding bottles of beer in our coat sleeves, talking each other down off ledges, and carving our initials (and those of the boys we would marry) into every visible surface.

Now we're cutting the crust off peanut butter sandwiches in different parts of the country. Coming from a small town, we all moved away after high school. We pursued different careers, fell in love with different people, and popped out a few rugrats like it ain't no thang. Now we see one another once or twice a year, for a few hours at best.

But geography can only take part of the blame. Kelly, one of my oldest childhood friends, lives just a couple minutes away. Twenty-five years ago, we would sit in her bedroom with her ghetto blaster and write out the lyrics to Bon Jovi songs.

"She says we've got to hold on to what we've got. It doesn't make a difference if we're naked or not."

"Shock to the heart and you're too late. You give love…a band-aid."

Now we're in our own separate living rooms listening to profound lyrics like "Who lives in a pineapple under the sea? Sponge. Bob. Square. Pants" and "Heroes in a half-shell…Turtle Power!" and helping our boys write their names on birthday cards. Birthday parties are the bane of our existence, but at least they force us to see each

other's face a few times a year. Not that we have much time for eye contact while we're wiping up juice puddles and keeping grubby hands off the presents.

We used to be friends first. Now, above all, we are parents. But at least Kelly and I understand each other. The childless crowd...not so much.

There are those friends without kids who either stop inviting us places because all we do is jabber about our youngsters and say super dickish things like, "You think that's bad? Just wait til you have kids." Or they just assume we can't make it, and they're probably right; not all of us have live-in nannies from the Philippines. If I'm packing up the little dude to go to Grandma's for the night or paying a sitter by the hour, it better be bloody worth it. You better be making fucking nachos. After the first dozen turndowns, or no reply at all because we're too busy wiping snotty noses to type a single sentence, we can't really blame them for giving up on us.

Then there are the childless morons who tell us to come to party and—what the heck—bring the kid! Just put him to bed upstairs while we get our drink on. Oh sure, Max will settle down just perfectly in your unfamiliar house of booze. He won't wake up a dozen times and fall over the perilous staircase into a living room full of shitfaced adults who can't drive him to the hospital. Great plan. I'll definitely be able to relax and enjoy myself at this shindig. Count me in, genius.

And then, of course, there are friends who are parents just like us. If we're not in different time zones, we're at least on different schedules. We are the executive assistants of our homemade VIPs, escorting them around with clipboards tucked under our arms, making sure they're on time, fuelled up, and dressed for the occasion. Doctor's appointments, birthday parties, swimming lessons, soccer, mealtime, naptime, bathtime, bedtime. By 10 p.m., we're reaching for the plug in the bathtub that we forgot to pull out hours ago, our heads drifting slowly forward with fatigue. What a noble way to die: ass up and facedown in six inches of stale bathwater. Good thing we didn't accept our friend's invite to the late movie. The entire Justice League combined could not stop this train wreck.

Everyone is busy. Everyone is tired. We're all doing the best we can. But what happens when we finally emerge from the abyss of parenthood? *Hey, where'd everybody go?* What happens when part of our nuclear family is compromised with sickness, heartache, or death? Sooner or later, we need to reach out for help, beyond the little circle we created when we became parents.

We could all learn a few things from my mom, other than how to clean the inside of a toaster. She has a cabinet full of "You're Special" and "Friends Forever" ornaments and figurines (which I better not inherit when she conks), given to her by friends to whom she has been so kind and generous. When Dad died, those friends returned the favour. They all brought food in great quantities. They were all there to hold her hand, just as she held theirs during trying times. Some of them were even right there at that very moment when Dad stopped breathing. And they've been there ever since. I mean they went home to shower and stuff, but you know what I mean. These friendships that she nurtured all her life, even through the mayhem of parenthood, took centre stage when she needed them most. Mom lives four hours away from me. So it's a great relief to know she's not alone. And that she doesn't have to move in with me anytime soon.

But friendships have been easier for Mom to maintain because she has lived in the same town pretty much all her life. The friends she made when she was younger, she's kept. Because nobody ever moved away. Calling them to catch up requires but a couple of tin cans and a string. It's not so easy for our generation of nomads. Our friends from childhood, high school, and college are all over the map. We'd have better luck connecting with the ghost of Elvis.

We've made some new friends, naturally. At work. At play groups. At cul-de-sac parties. At book club benders. People we've bonded with as adults and parents. I had a dozen co-workers show up at Dad's funeral after a four-hour drive in the dead of winter. It was a nice supplement to the small kindergarten crew, many of which had to send messages and marigolds in their stead.

I talk a big game, but when it comes down to it, I don't actually want *too many* friends. Not close friends. As wonderful as they are,

I just don't have the time to invest, and I'd rather not have a huge lineup of disgruntled wonderful people that I neglect and disappoint. Better to have a handful of rad peeps I can genuinely appreciate in small (because that's all I got right now, man) ways.

But even with that handful of friends, old or new, near or far, we still face the challenge of Zombie Parent Syndrome. We often can't think straight long enough to consciously decide to make more time for friendship. But somehow, we gotta snap out of it. When all the bread crusts are cut and the laundry is done, we're going to need each other. Because, while raising our kids is the biggest challenge of our lives, it's not the only one. And besides, it's not just about maintaining a good clean-up crew when you have a spill on aisle life. It's about setting an example for our kids on a regular basis. We're not just hanging out with our buddies to get away from the little punks for a spell. We're also teaching them a very important lesson: friendship is good.

Human Skittles

I went back to work a year after dropping the sprog. Max was one. Most daycare centres won't take 'em that young, so my aunt generously offered to watch him for me. Sometimes she even picked him up and fed him and stuff.

When he turned two, Andrew and I started thinking he should go to a daycare centre once or twice a week. You know, with other kids. So he'd know he's not a leprechaun. So I put Max on several waiting lists in the city, but it seemed he had a better chance of getting into Harvard. Ah well, I wasn't about to settle for a daycare in some old broad's smoky basement. I would hold out for the daycare of my dreams: a daycare with six or seven other children who are gentle, vaccinated, and cootie-free. Where one of the kids is Asian, and one of them black, and one of them is from Timbuktu—something super exotic to really mix shit up. What? I want to raise my child in a diverse community, okay? Which begs the question: why do I live in Torbay, Newfoundland?

The town's theme song is "A Whiter Shade of Pale." They don't even sell Oreos at the Foodland.

Growing up, I was fortunate to have a couple non-white families in our community. One from the Philippines, one from Laos, and a handful from other parts of Asia (doctors and their families, mostly. Shocker.) In spite of my small rural existence, I knew there was variety in the world; we weren't all pasty-as-my-arse honkies of English or Irish descent. It's okay, I can say the H word because I am one.

My friend Tina also had a black Baby Brenda doll. So we knew babies came in all colours. In fact, one Christmas during our church concert, we put Black Brenda in the manger to play the role of Jesus. The kids who were playing Mary and Joseph were as white as the driven snow, but no odds—this conception was immaculate. Gangsta God, the other Notorious B.I.G, was Jesus's baby daddy.

When they were toddlers, my friend Kelly took her twin boys to the swimming pool. They saw a black man treading water nearby and the boys started to panic. No, they didn't think they were going to get mugged or rapped at. The boys just hadn't seen a black person before! On another occasion, they were in the checkout line at the grocery store, standing behind a black man. One of the boys looked at his mother and said, quite loudly, "Why is that man's face so black?" Not sure what to say at the moment, Kelly shushed him. What the heck is the answer to this innocent inquiry anyways? "Because there are all kinds of people in the world, honey. Of all shapes and sizes and colours," or, "Because that man is clearly of African descent. I'll show you Africa on the map when we get home."

The hued dude overhears and interjects: "What're you gettin' on with? Sure, I'm from Dildo!"[3]

I'm not being racist. I love colour! I buy Max the box of *at least* sixty-four crayons. If you buy the pack of eight, you're practically pro-slavery. I want my son to experience diversity from an early age. Bring on the black kid, the aboriginal kid, the gay kid, the ginger

---

[3] Relax. Dildo is a picturesque little town in Trinity Bay, Newfoundland, about one hour from St. John's. If only penises were so pretty.

kid (check!), the kid with two moms, the kid in the wheelchair, the girl in the muslin dress, the boy who wears nail polish, the big-boned kid, and the kid with the robotic arm aka RoboKid. Come one and come all to Max Murphy's playhouse. Where there's no such thing as ignorance or hatred, and Cowboys and Indians will not be played.

Take Your Sperm and Shove It!

In September 2011, the *Globe and Mail* printed an article about a ginger seal in Russia. Shunned by its own mother and rejected by the seal colony for its unusual colour, a photographer spotted it hiding under some logs—blind, frightened, and all alone.

I'm happy to report this ginger mammal found a new home at a dolphinarium. Now, if only we could stop the discrimination of ginger humans! According to the *Globe and Mail* one week later, nobody wants redhead babies anymore. Cryos International, the world's largest sperm bank, is rejecting donations from redheads on account of low demand. Spread your seed elsewhere, Ginger Joe. Take your scarlet sperm and shove it—anywhere but in these women. These would-be baby makers don't want none of your red-hot lava love.

I know I'm not a dude, but I am a ginger. And frankly, this rejection hurts. In the words of Ron Burgundy, "I'm too hurt. I'm shocked and offended—and hurt."

Not really.

Cryos is just giving the market what they want in order to remain the world's biggest, awesomest turkey baster. The company has impregnated 18,731 women since 1991 and hope to knock up hundreds of thousands more. Cryos is also the Greek word for Arnold Schwarzenegger.

Nobody wants your lil' swimmers, generous gingers. Try the food bank. Or the bank bank. Or maybe a dolphinarium? Oh wait, Ireland wants you! Yay, Ireland! Redhead sperm sells in the Emerald Isle "like hotcakes," the director of Cryos says. I knew I should have been born to an Irish family. Instead of a freak, I'd have been a star, frolicking through the clovers while people threw Lucky Charms cereal at my freckles. Shag the Blarney Stone; people would want to bend over and kiss my sweet, snow-white ass.

But alas, the rest of the world sees things differently. They think we're fugly. Nothing new, I suppose. There's a Kick a Ginger Day for cryin' out loud. This news is just another kick in the pants to those poor redhead pervs who only get their rocks off at the sperm bank.

So it's true then. The ugly complex I had as a child was not all in my imagination. People—mothers!—don't want redhead babies because they think redheads are unattractive, or they think the chances of Adult-Onset Ugliness are far greater when you're born a redhead.

Piss poor logic, ladies! Granted, there are some unsightly redheads out there. But we're such a small fragment of the population. You notice our imperfections more because you notice *us* more! We're unique! We stand out, good-looking and butt-fugly alike. What about all those Lyle Lovett brunettes and Tori Spelling blondes. Come on, they are *everywhere*! Your chances of an ugly kid are just as high, no matter what colour hair graces the noggin of your baby daddy. Maybe you should worry about the hideous contents of that egg in your abdomen. Maybe that's enough ugly for everybody, gurlfren.

I blame the literature of yore for the bad rap: *Little Orphan Annie*, *Anne of Green Gables*, *Pippi Longstocking*. All poor, raggedy-ass rejects without parents, without an inkling of sexuality. I had more than one Halloween costume in the likeness of the aforementioned. One Halloween, I didn't dress up at all and people said, "Oh, let me guess… Raggedy-Ann?"

Go fuck yourself.

No wonder I hated my hair growing up. Two reasons:

1. Some people called me Carrot Top, to which I replied, without fail, "Carrot tops are green, beyotch!" (Or whatever we said before beyotch was invented by crossing a bitch with a crotch.) Idiots. Then the ridicule evolved into Fire Crotch. At least that was kind of clever. Kudos.

2. The haircuts inflicted upon me by my mother. She clearly hated me. Her weapon of choice? Scissors. I believe one time she also used a bowl—plopped it on my head and trimmed around it like she was cutting excess pastry from the edge of a pie plate. The cruelty did not cut too deeply though, because it was also endured by my brother.

Misery loves company. I had hockey hair. Short in the front with a dust ruffle at the back. But we both had the dreaded Danny Williams[4] split. Our heads looked like furry, orange Muppet asses. (I can't even talk about the wardrobe. Or Glenn's freakishly gigantic hand.)

I prayed to the gods to grant me a more magnetic mane. And then, somewhere in my teenage years, my prayer was answered. And with it came a flurry of hormonal freshmen trying to see if the carpet matched the drapes. Ugh.

It's all about the product, baby. I can tell you my secrets in exchange for your first-born child. As long as it's not a redhead. Nice try; I ain't taking that reject off your hands.

Okay I'll stop being a crazy bitch now (it's the savage ginge in me). Truth is, I totally get it! You're barren. Or you're a lesbian. It's all good. You and your spouse don't have red hair (only 3% of the population does), so why would you select that trait in your male-order baby? Understood. I mean, if you're a brunette/blonde couple and your kid is born with red hair, people will think a third party was involved.

But guess what, genetics is a bitch. You might wind up with a ginger out of sheer luck (or retribution), because unbeknownst to you, your lil' ol' egg could be brimming with the nectar of the ginger gods. Muhahahahaha…

Come on redheads, let's breed! Let's not let the dwindling ginger population die of rejection. (But don't count on me—because of the whole vagina massacre thing.) Don't let this sperm-bank nonsense discourage you. Stay the course on Copperhead Road. Go

---

4 Danny Williams, premier of Newfoundland and Labrador from 2005-2010, always wore his hair parted in the middle.

find your Prince Harry or your Christina Hendricks and lock those ginger crotches. Squirt your scarlet juice into the wind until it sticks! Do whatever it takes to keep our kind alive, and one day sweet victory shall be ours: total global ginger domination.

Shit That Blows My Mind

They say motherhood makes you stupid. Forgetful. What was I saying? They say giving birth gives you "baby brain." Reduced mental capacity. I concur. I mean, I think I concur. Where am I? What's happening?

When Max was barely walking, I locked myself out of the house while wearing my slippers and big pink bathrobe. Max could see me through the window and started to cry. I tore off up the street to get some help. Picture a tumbleweed of cotton candy staggering into the local mechanic's shop. As one of the employees followed me back to the house, it must have looked like a scene from a horror movie: distraught woman in bathrobe and slippers running down the street pursued by man in coveralls holding an enormous pipe-wrench. He beat the doorknob off in one swift swing, and I rushed in to comfort my boy. Then he said I didn't need to pay him for his service if I let him try on my cocktail dresses and high-heel shoes. Actually, I think I'm getting him mixed up with someone else. The details are fuzzy. I have baby brain.

Okay, so I'm more absentminded than ever. But I *think* more clearly. I really do. It's just that some things in this life I just can't quite grasp in my big fuzzy head. Here is a short list of those things.

BABIES COME FROM OUR VAGINAS. Our *vaginas*. I just can't wrap my head around it (though it has been wrapped around a head). The fact that they use forceps, a vacuum, or a knife to *extract* the baby half the damn time tells me there has to be a better way to do this. But oh no, it's gotta be the ol' pickle jar. Quite the hub of activity down there. And yet women keep spittin' out babies left and right like it's small potatoes, just as they have for thousands of years.

YAWNS. They're contagious. Don't deny it. Can someone please explain this to me in scientific (but not too scientific, I'm an English major) terms? I need answers. And I'm tired (yawn) of waiting (yawn). You're yawning now too, aren't you? Aren't you?

THE SCOPE OF THE UNIVERSE. Have you any idea just how insignificant we are? Imagine a microscopic particle on the hair on the pimple on an elephant's ass on the elephant on the tree in the hole in the bog down in the valley-o, and then divide that by eighty-seven gazillion trillion jajillion. That's how un-big you are in the grand scope of things.

ANIMAL INSTINCTS. How does a baby horse just slide out of its mama and, within minutes, know how to walk? Did he take a tutorial in utero? How do salmon know their way back to their native rivers? And how a common house pet can find its way home from great distances is truly astounding. My grandfather used to walk from Cape Freels to Gambo (a seventy-five-minute drive by car today, a multi-day trek by foot back in the day) to catch the train to St. John's with his loyal mutt by his side. When he arrived in Gambo, he traded the dog for some tobacco. When he returned from the seal hunt several weeks later, the dog would be back in Cape Freels again, having left its new owner and found its way home. That ol' dog was a gift that kept on giving.

SCROTUMS. If it wants so badly to have sex, couldn't it have been even mildly attractive? Even on a twenty-year-old stud, it looks like an old man's jowl flap.

BIGOTRY. It blows my mind that, in this day and age, there are still people who hate blacks and gays. Get over it already. Your hate could be put to much greater use on rapists, pedophiles, and people who rush to be first in line when a new cash opens at the grocery store. Die! Die! Die!

MIRRORS. Think about it. Now think about it backwards.

The Lord Made Me
but the Devil Raised Me

We used to own a gun.

A little, plastic novelty gun that gave you a shock when you pulled the trigger. It was a source of entertainment for weeks as we tried to get unsuspecting visitors, even the kids, to squeeze the trigger.

Max was the last to fall for it. (Turbo Ginger ain't no fool.) I expected him to drop the gun and do his trademark *owwww* with a couple crocodile tears for dramatic effect. To our surprise, Max is a sadomasochist. He kept pulling the trigger again and again, flinching his eyes then grinning, enjoying the little charge of electricity coursing through his wee finger.

Mix messages much? Here we were encouraging our child to play with a toy gun. In our next breath, we're telling him guns are the devil. "Here, Max, take this toy gun and shoot Grandma. Good job, son! And now for your reward: a Popeye cigarette! Go ahead, pretend you're having a draw. But remember, smoking is Satan. Hey, wanna play *Call of Duty* in a greasy white tank top?"

Max still sometimes uses his pants as a toilet, so I don't expect him to know the difference between a gun that's a toy and one that can blow your fuckin' brains out. But hey, it's not like he'll ever have the chance to pull the trigger on a real gun before he knows the difference, right? This ain't Texas. If the husband ever buys a shotgun for moose hunting, it will be stored in a locked steel case, in a chained-up iron box, in a room with a force field around it, on Jupiter. Seriously though, there's no 9 mm semi-automatic lying around Chez Murphy. And besides, toy guns don't make your kids grow up to be cowboys. Or criminals. If they did, my brother'd be wearing assless chaps (more often) and blowing people's kneecaps off with an AK-47.

The batteries in the toy gun expired around the same time Nicholas Winsor did. Perhaps you've forgotten him already. I have not. A couple years back, his picture was all over the news. Tough guy, 120 pounds soaking wet, covered in tattoos. And oh yeah, he's also dead, but in the press his death seemed secondary to how he looked and how he lived.

It was spring of 2011. The twenty-year-old St. John's man took a fatal gunshot to the neck. Two of his best buddies will now stand trial for second-degree murder after an altercation that went bad. If this were a big city, it'd be just one of many such incidents on the daily news. But this is not Toronto or LA or Baghdad. Around here, stuff like this makes headlines and shakes us to the core.

I have to admit—the tattoos made me roll my eyes and shake my head. I think there was one collective glare of disgust and premature conviction across the city when we saw their photos: the now deceased in his invincible gangster stance with "Trust No One" inked on his forearms. One of the alleged shooters with teardrops etched on his face. (Max could have done a better job with his jumbo crayons.) And on the neck of the other alleged perp, the words that inspired the title of this section: "The Lord made me but the devil raised me." I doubt his parents put that artwork on the fridge.

Sorry for the prejudice all you good, law-abiding people with tats on your faces and necks, but Max is never getting a tattoo. Unless it says "Rainbows Rule" or "Get your pet spayed or neutered" or "I love my mom."

My initial reaction? These boys are lost causes. I felt little more pity for the dead guy as I did for the shooters. A gun went off. It could have been any of the lot. There was no victim here. Just look at their Facebook pics: hard tickets posing with homemade shanks in what looks like a jailhouse scene. What a waste of life. The victim's and the alleged shooters' alike.

But that was my fear talking. What if Max were in the wrong place at the wrong time? Bang, you're dead, beautiful little boy. And in an instant my whole world is snuffed out like a cheap candle.

What if Max grows into a shy, awkward kid and finds acceptance with "the wrong crowd"?

What if he has a darkness inside him? Something he was born with, a mental condition and a predisposition for trouble. What if some kids are just born bad? What if it's completely out of my hands? Now…where's that toddler-sized bubble I bought on e-bay?

I think back to when Max was born. An eight-pound bundle of possibility. He didn't ask to be born. He came to be, because of his father's inability to resist my womanly form. And now his whole existence is in our hands. I remember walking out of the hospital with the car seat, thinking, *Are they really going to just let us walk out of here with this person? Aren't they going to give us a psych test or something, a skill-testing question at least?*

We are his everything. The be-all and end-all. For a good portion of his life, we hold all the cards. We determine the outcome. It's a lot of responsibility, and a lot of power.

Nick Winsor was somebody's bundle once, too. He didn't ask to be born. When he was a little boy and someone asked him what he wanted to be when he grew up, he didn't say a gun-slinging gangster. He probably wanted to be a firefighter or a truck driver or—oh the irony—a police officer. I don't blame his mother or his father because I don't know the whole story. Maybe they did the best they knew how. Maybe Nick just found himself in a bad situation. Nobody knows for sure. As a mother myself, I have compassion for the woman he called Mom, no matter how she raised him. No mother deserves to see her child pieced back together in a coffin, while she falls apart every day for the rest of her life.

Surely this case will make headlines again when the trial begins. So next time you see the face of Nick Winsor on your TV or computer screen, look beyond the tattoos and the tough guy bullshit. You'll see a scared little boy, poorly equipped for a big world.

Granted, I want Max to stay the hell away from boys who act all tough, who succumb to the attraction of certain negative male stereotypes. But I also want Max to have compassion. So I must have compassion, too. Childhood is a critical time. It makes you or it breaks you. So all of us who have remained intact: let's have a heart for the broken. Luck is never distributed evenly or fairly.

I look at Max and wonder what the future holds. To borrow a line from *Mad Men*'s Don Draper on the birth of his son, "We don't know who he is yet or who he is going to be, and that is a wonderful thing." I don't know how Max will turn out, but I do know I will try my damnedest to keep him on the good path. Because obviously the bad path is just around the corner from our house. And if it ever rises up to meet my precious boy, I will beat the shit out of it with a shovel. Which I keep under my bed. So I can bury would-be kidnappers right after I whack them.

Dear Pope: Time for a Few Tweaks

How do you prevent a mommy blogger from ringing in the New Year in head-to-toe flannel, scraping chocolate out of her spacebar with a label from a bottle of cheap wine while she updates her Facebook status to: "The first person to bring me another bottle of Shiraz wins a big, fat prize wrapped in flannel"?

Invite her to a wedding.

Congratulations to the newlyweds, Jake and Amy.[5] What a lovely couple. Jake…what a handsome husband. And Amy…what a perfect lampstand. WTF? Let me explain.

This is the reading they chose—I repeat, *chose*—for the church nuptials. Allow me to quote from the Book of Sirach:

> Happy is the husband of a good wife; the number of his days will be doubled. A loyal wife brings joy to her husband, and he will complete his years in peace. A good wife is a great blessing; she will be granted among the blessings of the man who fears the Lord. Whether rich or poor, his heart is content, and at all times his face is cheerful.
>
> A wife's charm delights her husband, and her skill puts flesh on his bones. A silent wife is a gift from the Lord, and nothing is so precious as her self-discipline. A modest wife adds charm to charm, and no scales can weigh the value of her chastity. Like the sun rising in the heights of the Lord, so is the beauty of a good wife in her well-ordered home. Like the shining lamp on the holy lampstand, so is a beautiful face on a stately figure. Like golden pillars on silver bases, so are her shapely legs and steadfast feet.

---

5   Their names were not Jake and Amy. I had to change their real names in my **HuffPost** article after the bride received several phone calls from disgruntled members of the Pope fan club. Sorry for the trouble "Amy," and thanks for the material.

One second. I need to go flip the flapjacks, then iron my husband's shirts, then "add charm to charm," then hurl. All the while remaining cheerfully silent and glowing like a shining lamp.

I'm not sure if the passage was read verbatim. I was too busy picking my jaw off the floor, pinching myself, and mentally slapping my husband who kept looking at me with that smug "Get in the kitchen and make me some pie" look.

The thoughts kept pinballing around in my head:

Is this really happening?

Did he really just say that?

Is this 1954?

Is the Pope a He-Man Woman Hater?

What's next—a pro-slavery poem?

Someone check my ears for wax. There must be a full box of crayons in there because what I'm hearing just can't be right.

I'm not a hard-core feminist. Not intentionally, at least. Sometimes I even objectify myself. (The red dress I wore to the wedding was purchased at Trollops.) But what in the name of Christ (that's not a curse—I mean it literally) is this verbiage doing within a one hundred yard radius of a Christian establishment?

So let me get this straight. The Catholic Church thinks that, to be a good wife, I need to be a good housekeeper? Someone interpret that differently for me. Please. Be my guest. Tell me I'm reading it all wrong. I will gladly accept dyslexia in exchange for clarity that does not involve me wearing an apron around my "stately figure" in my "well-ordered home."

I wonder if the Pope has a little diagram of a "good wife" pinned to his fridge (full of wine and unleavened bread?) of a shapely (but modest!) woman holding a feather duster, bending over (but not too far!) to wipe the crud off her husband's big, long briefcase that contains his big, long list of manly achievements.

Seriously. Is this Holy Scripture or last month's copy of *Hustler*? But hey, this gibber-jabber was written a couple thousand years ago. I can't blame the Church today for something written in another time. But I *can* tsk-tsk today's Church for offering up that passage as an appropriate reading for a marriage! Dudes—there are so many other passages, why include this one in the list? Leave that one in the dark ages from whence it came. Keep it locked up in the closet with the rest of the secrets. We women are trying to get ahead here. Do a girl a solid, would ya?

Thankfully, the Protestants do not accept the scripture of Sirach. High five, Anglicans! And an additional low five for allowing women to preach. I mean of course Catholic women can't preach; they're too busy sharpening their "skills," to put meat on their husbands' bones. Holy hilarious. Even the priest who officiated the marriage made amendments for this dinosaur of an excerpt. After the reading, he chuckled and said something like, "Of course, all these things can be applied to the husband as well." I breathed a sigh of relief. At least he kinda-sorta acknowledged the hogwashiness of the thing.

With all due respect, Mr. Pope, it's time for a few updates. Kick that passage to the curb. The Bible is, like, a gazillion pages long; surely you have enough other sacred stuff to draw from. Maybe this bullshit seemed acceptable (acceptable, but not right) through to the 1950s, but come on—times have changed a little, don't you think? The leader of the free world is black. The Chancellor of Germany, the fourth most powerful economy in the world, is a woman. Scientists at CERN think they have finally found the Higgs boson.[6] Poodle skirts are museum pieces, telephones don't have cords, and you can't slap a woman's ass in the office anymore without getting slapped back with a civil suit.

Come on, Francis, I know you're not that out of touch. I'm following you on Twitter, for god's sake! Now…why can't women be priests? Are we ladies not capable of being divine? Is our divinity restricted to our partridgeberry pie and how we fold those blasted fitted sheets with the elastic at the corners? Let us in. Not me, hells no, but anyone else with girl parts who wants in. Why not? Oh, and while you're at it, maybe you could re-word the whole thing about homosexuality being a "disorder." That's just silly.

---

[6] The Higgs Boson is blah blah blah physics blah blah electromagnetic force word word word big bang blah blah elusive god particle. Look—it was impossible to find but they found it, okay? Times have changed.

I think most priests and churchgoers would agree—congregations (and, consequently, contributions to the collection plate) are dwindling as communities age. The Church is a dying institution as more and more young people drift further and further away from conventional religion. So helloooooo—if you are trying to appeal to a younger, modern demographic, this is so not the way to do it. Maybe it's time to wake up and consider that maybe your "New" Testament is really fucking old.

When I heard that reading during the wedding ceremony, I thought to myself: thank god (not really) that I was married by the town mayor because this backwards baloney is just bananas. I'm sure there are other teachings and readings that I could embrace on principle, and many that I already do, but the endorsement of this Sirach poppycock is enough to turn me toward voodoo.

Go ahead. Put me on the Illuminaughty List. Until there's an update, I will continue to worship the fairies in the woods. Word.

And to all ye getting married in the Catholic Church, for the love of god and all his creatures great and small and male and female, stick with Corinthians. Yes, we're tired of hearing that crap too, but at least faith, hope, and love don't make anyone feel like a lampstand.

A Letter to Max

Mommy bloggers get slammed a lot. We're either too corny or too crass. We're either exploiting our kids or being too guarded and, therefore, not connecting to our audience. If we talk about trivial family stuff, we're weaklings, and giving the rest of the poor damsels a bad name too. And obviously, we're all extreme narcissists. I mean, how dare we write about *ourselves* on the Internet? For shame.

We just can't win. So let's just shut the fuck up and go back to the kitchen and grate some cheese, because writing is nacho thing, mama. You can't be everything to everyone, so strive to be nothin' to nobody except a good little wife to your man and the perfect little mommy to your children.

FUCK THAT SHIT. It's a free country. Write about whatever you want! World peace or peas and carrots. How to toilet-train a cat or how to knit a baby hat. Get on it like a bonnet. Thing is, if a mom blogs about nothing but bonnets, that doesn't mean bonnets are her world. It means *she blogs about bonnets.* For all we know, she could be a rocket scientist politician supermodel serial killer, who happens to make bonnets. Even if her blog is an abomination in the blogosphere, at least she's doing something besides filing her nails.

Since I started blogging, I've gotten quite a bit of feedback. Lots and lots of love (my only form of income thus far), and a loving handful of total and utter crazeballs. I've been called evil, insensitive, judgmental, misinformed, anti-feminist, and feminist (how is this even an insult?). Clearly, to be a writer, especially one writing about the sacred vocation of motherhood, you need to have a really, really, really thick skin. And not just inside your love taco.

Some commenters said they wanted to adopt Max to save him from his cold, cruel mother. No need for formal adoption, I told them. They could have him for twenty bucks and a six-pack.

Some say I talk about motherhood too lightly, like it's a game. Really? Motherhood is not a game? And all this time I thought I was playing Hungry Hungry Hippos. You have to admit though, this *is* a lot like Monopoly. Some dude lands in your Free Parking and the next thing you know you're begging for a get-out-of-jail-free card.

Some people say I'm exploiting Max by writing about him without his permission. That's just not true. When he was an infant, I asked him if it was okay to blog about him and I swear he nodded his head. He shook his rattle too, like a tambourine cheering me on.

Look, maybe they're right. Maybe one day I'll wake up with writer's remorse and regret every page. But I can only be who I am *now* and know what I know *now.* And right now, this is it. Love it or leave it on the counter of a second-hand bookstore.

In any case, I'm prepared. I'm saving for Max's therapy, and one day if he needs a little extra help to deal with his mother's maniacal musings, I've written him this letter:

Dear Max:

One day, one of your evil classmates is going to bring this book to school, hand it to you, and say, "Page 11 is all about your mom's vagina." In fact, I probably just guaranteed this will indeed happen.

It's okay if you're embarrassed. Children are supposed to be ashamed of their parents, especially when those parents are really funny and awesome. But when that kid says his mom says *your* mom is "crazy" or "vulgar" or a "bad mom," you make sure to reply with one of the following:

1. Oh yeah, well at least my mom can write more than her name on a bathroom stall.

2. At least my mom *has* a vagina. I heard your mom's got an alpaca farm down there.

3. Your mom is just jealous because your dad wishes my mom was your mom.

4. That ol' thing? That's what my mom was doing while working and parenting and blogging and playing football and saving the whales and stuff. What does your mom do, other than change your big-boy diapers and bleach her moustache?

Now you're all set. Of course, the best thing to do is just smile and say, "Tell your mom thanks so much for buying a copy. I'm one step closer to Disney World. Again."

With all my love,
Mom

P.S. I'm very proud of you, even if you're not proud of me (yet).

There is a crack, a crack in everything.
That's how the light gets in.

— LEONARD COHEN, "ANTHEM"

CHAPTER EIGHT

Oh Shit We're All Going to Die

Mom kept a stack of sympathy cards in the top drawer of her dresser, beneath her big satin underwear. They fascinated me. The cards, not the underwear. Why did she have so many of them? Did she buy them in bulk? Was she expecting a mass murder? Was she *planning* a mass murder?

It's no wonder I was obsessed with death. Like the guy from *Superbad* who draws cocks all day long, I wrote poems about death 24/7. And yes, a scattered verse about cock. All in my glossy pink diary with the lock and key. I don't have any of the old gems now, but I suspect they sounded a lot like this:

> There once was a frog.
> He sat on a log.
> The log was full of splinters.
> He croaked.

Or,

> Roses are red.
> Death is black.
> Poems are hard.
> Death.

Man, that's deep.

With time, life imitated my so-called art. My frog didn't die, but the people around me started to. My friend's dad was killed in a car accident when we were just five years old. My grandmother keeled over when I was thirteen. And shortly thereafter, my friend's dad succumbed to cancer. Then my grandfather died. Then River Phoenix. Then Kurt Cobain. Then Tupac. Then Lady Diana. Geez, who was next—Michael Jackson? Whitney Houston? It was only a matter of time before death was on the doorstep of the house of Combden. Like a reality show inspired by one of my twisted poems.

In 2008, the Grim Reaper came knockin'. First for Mom then Dad. Breast cancer and colon cancer, respectively. Their diagnoses were less than a year apart.

Suddenly, I became acutely aware of the temporariness of everything. Nobody's getting out of this world alive. Not even Oprah. We're all fucked. And I am especially fucked with cancer gyrating through my DNA. I developed a need to do everything as soon as possible. No more procrastination. Make my dreams come true before I stop waking up from them. I needed to write a book, travel the world, take up golf, but first—have a baby.

No Bunny's Daughter

Father's Day is pretty much as you'd expect for someone whose father is dead. It's like Valentine's Day when you're single, times a hundred-thousand-million. Because at least you can find new love; you only get one dad. Unless your dads are gay so you have two. You get my point.

Up until the dark day, on every Father's Day for as long as I can remember, I gift-wrapped yet another jumbo pack of golf balls, a silly poem, and a pack of gum.

No more. Callaway and Top-Flite sales have plummeted since Jim Combden permanently retired his clubs.

"Take a look at me now. There's just an empty space. Nothing left here to remind me...," except all the happy people celebrating their dads who are so awesome and wonderful and, oh yeah, *alive*!

Now Father's Day is just a shot in the guts, reminding me (as if I don't already know and think about it daily) that mine is gone. I once again blame Hallmark for inventing a holiday to sell corny, overpriced greeting cards without considering how much it costs to send a card to heaven. One stamp costs sixty cents and your goddamn soul.

Ironically, when I was a kid, Dad used to feign death for entertainment purposes. It was one of his go-to pranks that never got old. I'd come home from school to find him lying there on the floor, his hands perfectly crossed on his chest, his trademark smirk on his face. It's still funny, in spite of today's reality.

Speaking of Hallmark, and speaking of pranks, I wish I'd get a card in the mail with a great big "GOTCHA!" on the inside. These past couple of years, maybe Dad has just been punking us, hiding in the bushes on the eleventh hole of the Gander Golf Course. Negator. Dad never could hold back a punchline.

Father's Day: blah.

But then I saw the rabbits.

I was on my way to the Relay for Life, where I would be doing laps around a gym for twelve hours to help fight cancer in honour of dear old Dad. Just after I had taken the ramp to get off the TCH, two brown bunnies darted across the street right in front of my car. One on the heels of the other, they scurried into the thick greenery and were gone.

They say your sense of smell is the sense most linked to memory. I close my eyes and I can still smell the Tinkerbell make-up in my jewelry box with the creepy twirling ballerina, and my scrumptious Strawberry Shortcake figurines, and the scratch and sniff stickers in my sticker book (mmm, grape). But most of all, I can still smell the rabbits.

Clinging to the back of our old black and green Jag Arctic Cat, I watched Dad lumber through the waist-deep snow to check his snares for rabbits. The unlucky furballs were soon dangling from the beams of his shed, frozen in their last earthly stance, paws pointing in all directions. The next day, they'd still be hanging there, stripped of their fur down to the purple, sinewy muscle. The shed smelled perpetually of rabbits. Even in the summer, it hung in the air. Was it the stench of death, or fur, or raw meat? I'm not sure. To me, it's the smell of a happy childhood.

But these rabbits on the highway were free and fast and full of life. And instead of one lonely rabbit, there were two. I instantly thought of Dad. Was he speaking to me on this day before Father's Day, as I was about to go kick some carcinogenic ass? On the way home the next morning, when St. John's was barely awake, I again saw a sign: a dove! Okay, that's a lie. It was a white plastic bag flapping around in the wind. But it had a life about it. An *American Beauty*[1] if you will. You know the scene.

Oh come on. Who am I kidding? Dad is not speaking to me from the great beyond. He's not sending me messages from a Voodoo Lounge in the clouds with Hemingway throwing back shots at the bar and Shakespeare practicing his bank shot in the far corner. He's not showing me the beauty in the world. I'm finding it myself because he taught me how. I see things more clearly than ever through the eyes that he gave me.

Guess we should teach our children well. Not by instruction, but by example. Actions speak louder than words, and lessons last much longer than the human body.

And our kids are not the only ones picking up what we're laying down. I can only imagine how many students Dad inspired during his thirty years of teaching English literature. Knowing Dad was extremely sick, one of his students sent him a thank-you note to express how much he had inspired her. Her note arrived ten minutes too late. Ten minutes. But I got to read it, so it was not entirely in vain. And Dad knew she had become an English teacher herself, so he probably suspected that he played some small part.

We are mere mortals. But the light we emit is absorbed by others and continues to shine long after our candle has burnt out. Wow, that's some cheesy metaphornication there, Elton John. Let's try it again with less fromage. My dad saw deep meaning in ordinary things. He talked about it. He wrote about it. Some called him a weirdo, some called him a poet. He put it all out there, fearlessly. And

---

[1] One of the most famous scenes from the Oscar-winning movie, *American Beauty*, featured a white, plastic bag blowing around in the wind.

I saw it. Every day. So even though he's gone, I see the beauty. There is still goodness. There is still humour. There is still life (not a bunch of fruit in a bowl—you know what I mean, saucy face). Because of what I learned from him, largely by simple observation, I am well-equipped to find reasons to be happy in this fucked-up, fatherless world.

Cock-a-Doodle-Dead

How much cock do you get on Mother's Day? Last year, I got four.

Well for starters, my husband had nothing to do with it; in fact, he went playing with his own balls.[2] Max got me out of bed before eight. Then the dog threw up. And before I knew it I was vacuuming, which is against the Supreme Law of Mother's Day. The day was off to a sucky start indeed.

But suckage turned to surprise when I went to the door to put the dog out. On my front deck were four roosters. Yes, roosters, like on the Kellogg's Corn Flakes box, except not the illustrated kind. They scattered in a hurry when Splash came bolting out. And thank goodness; there is no way I'm getting pregnant right now.

My encounters with birds did not stop there. A couple mornings later, I had another run-in. Literally.

I was cruising along the winding road out of Pouch Cove after dropping Max off at the sitter's when—*clunk*—I hit a bird. Was it a sparrow? Did god see it fall? Did it meet his tender view? Frig, I don't know, but he sure didn't save the little fella. It was a little teeny one from what I could gather. I saw him fly out of the trees on the left-hand side of the road, right into the grill of my car. I held my breath and looked in my side mirror, hoping to see him flying away into the wild blue yonder all hunky-dory. *Please let him be okay, please let him be okay.* But all I saw was the flutter of tiny wings on the pavement.

I contemplated pulling over, going back, giving him chest

[2] Golfing

compressions with my pinky finger and mouth-to-beak resuscitation. But I was already late for work, and what was I going to do anyway? Put him in a box and take him to the office? Feed him little bits of shredded paper and staple his wing back together with the stapler I stole from our Halifax office that time? What if he were hanging onto life by a single feather? Would I have to put him out of his misery? There's no way I could do it; I can't even pick a scab off a fly-bite. As I kept on driving, I imagined the little dude getting squished by the very next car or plucked up by a big scavenging seagull. I don't know what became of him. But one thing is clear. I am a horrible person.

So my day was off to a killer start. In an effort to forgive myself, I decided to be prepared for the next time it happens. When I arrived at work, I immediately googled "what to do with a broken bird." Wrong choice of keywords, let me tell you. There are some sick fucks out there. So I tried "helping an injured bird" and found a whole nest of information on the subject. Thanks Internets machine; now I know what to do! *eHow* also told me how to care for baby birds, how to capture an injured pelican, how to pluck a turkey, how to make a down comforter, and how to make a feather pen. I shit you not.

Why did this shattered bird weigh so heavily on me? I guess it's the doggy mama in me. Ever since Splash came into my world a few years ago, I have compassion for all creatures, great and small. I mean seriously, what is the difference? Who says my Portuguese water dog is worth more than a little sparrow? Well, the $1,600 price tag. But otherwise, what's the diff? If Splash was hurt and lying in the middle of the road, I'd call 9-1-1 and try my damnedest to convince the paramedics that she is a really hairy human with four legs. Hey, it's possible; pollution is causing all kinds of mutations these days.

I'd do that for my dog. Any dog, in fact. But not a bird, apparently.

The baby mama in me is that angel on my shoulder, telling me what to do (although clearly I don't always listen). I would want Max to help an animal if he saw one in distress. Unless it was a sabre-tooth tiger, in which case shag calling the vet; call the Museum of Science because someone's about to get famous. All jokes aside, I can't imagine an attribute I value more than kindness. Screw the wit, the athleticism, the courage, the smarts. If Max is kind to others, generous, and compassionate, I will be oh so proud of him. As long as he's also good-looking.

Also contributing to my sunken feeling was the fact that Dad loved birds. I gave him many a birdhouse for many a birthday. The trees were so full of them, our front yard looked like a postcard from a Greek village. So when I hit the bird that morning, I felt like I hit Dad. And he's already dead for god's sake. Double dead. Not cool. The self-loathing continues.

That's it. I'm going to put a shoebox in the car with a teeny tiny blanket in it, and some sticks and leaves, and maybe a worm. And some mud for the worm, so he doesn't die. But what if I have to feed the worm to a sick birdie? The poor little worm is a goner. Damn this food chain; I just can't win.[3]

Life Is a (Little Boy on a) Beach

When you have a baby, you need one thing: a camera. With video and photo capabilities. Not for the taping of the actual birth; that's just gross. For the moments that come after. You know, once you've put your bladder and asshole back inside your body cavity.

Oh, and there's one other thing you need when you have a baby. Someone to have it for you instead.

You need a camera and camcorder—because your memory is fucked. And because you need to capture the excitement, the big smiles, the insufferable cuteness, and the hilarious pants-on-your-head and naked-arse stuff. That shit is gold.

But capture the serene stuff too, to remind you that this state of mind does exist. It might just save your life.

These moments, like on days when I take Max to the beach, make me all poetic in the pants:

---

[3] In spite of my animal affections, like a proud Newfoundlander I support the seal hunt. Mostly by not thinking about the cute little furry ones. So stop calling me, Pamela.

To see a world in a grain of sand,
And heaven in a wild flower,
Hold infinity in the palm of your hand,
And eternity in an hour.

What did William Blake mean? Don't look at me; it's not like I studied Honours English at Dalhousie University[4] or anything, pfffft. But if I were to guess, he meant that the only heaven is right here on earth. In this sand that stretches as far as my eye can see. In the wild primrose poking their heads out of the rippled sand dunes. In this little hand I hold in mine, breaking free so he can scurry up the beach and touch a...

"Oh, Jesus, no, Max, stop—PUT DOWN THAT JELLYFISH!"

Blake meant life is beautiful. Not what comes after it. Screw the afterlife. Look at the here-and-now life. Ain't it purdy? But hey, what do I know? Take my interpretation with a grain of sand.

I believe that these are the moments, baby. The sound of the ocean and the squishy-squack of Max's sandals as he toddles along the beach. The solitary squeak of pedals in need of grease as he learns to ride his tricycle on a windless Sunday morning.

These moments are captured on tape, so I can revisit them, and restore what sanity I have left. This footage is priceless. If my house was burning and I only had room in my arms to carry a few things, I'd take the footage first. You know, after the kid and the dog and my favourite Levi's.

I have footage of my dad doing an inappropriate dance while holding a jar of peanut butter at his crotch, captured during some impromptu filming as he fixed himself a sandwich in the kitchen. He was full of joy and hope, in spite of the cancer. In the video, in fact, you can see the little bottle of chemo in a sling around his neck—the apparatus that administered the treatment through the port-a-cath in his chest.

That jar-crotch shimmy is one of my most valuable possessions. Seriously. If someone robbed us and was bolting down the street

---

[4] I graduated from Dalhousie University in 2000 with a BA: major in English, minor in binge drinking.

toward the getaway car with my DVDs and external hard drive, I'd be yelling after him: "Get back here, buddy! You've got my dead dad's crotch dance there—I need that back! Here, take all my diamonds, just give me the crotch dance!"

But here's the trick with constantly wielding a camera: you can't be so caught up in capturing the moment that you forget to be *in* the moment. Being an ad woman, always trying to find the picture-perfect shot, I'm guilty of this. But I'm aware of my tendency toward aesthetic obsession, so I host my own intervention whenever I get out of hand: "Dear Self, you have negatively impacted my life in the following ways…blah blah, yadda yadda. If you don't stop this behaviour, I'm done with you. Now hand over the camera." (I smugly pass the camera from right hand to left.) "That's not what I meant and you know it, Self! Gawd, you're so selfish."

I need to be present. I need to see what is happening right now, not what it will look like projected onto my living-room walls in twenty years. So I don't find myself watching a home movie ten years from now, wishing I had just dropped everything and run full-tilt down that beach toward the jellyfish instead of screaming, troll-voiced, behind the camera, "Fix his pants—I can see his diaper!"

Letting Go and Holding On

I sit here staring at two big boxes of books. Books I've toted around for more than a decade, from province to province and house to house. Damn, books are heavy. Time to lose some paperweight.

What was I thinking? Look at these titles. *Criminals, Idiots, Women and Minors: Victorian Writing by Women on Women.* How did I even pass that women's studies course? My brain twisted into a pretzel just reading the title.

The husband calls me a hoarder. (Better than whore, I suppose.) This, from a guy whose prized possession is a collection of over 200 beer bottles which adorn the walls of our basement. There are brown bottles in the background of every photo from Max's second birthday party. I'm surprised Social Services has not come a knockin'. I keep my mouth shut about the bottles; I've surrendered the basement in exchange for his manhood.

Maybe I am a packrat. But some things are simply not trash. These books, for example. You can't throw a book in the garbage. That's just *wrong*. To innovate on my mother's go-to guilt-inducer when I was a child: "Tsk tsk. All those children in Ethiopia with nothing to [read]…shockin'." (There was no Africa. There was only Ethiopia.)

Besides, no matter how awesome e-readers are, there is just something irreplaceably cool about a book of the paper kind. Like filmmaker John Waters said, "If you go home with somebody, and they don't have books, don't fuck 'em."

But for many of these volumes, the end has come. As much as I love the mildewy smell of their yellowing pages, they take up too much room in my bungalow and my life. Besides, just because you *own* a book does not mean you've read it. It's not like I can proudly stack them all on a shelf and wear a cigar jacket while I tell visitors how sophisticated and well-read I am: "I have many leather-bound books and my apartment smells of rich mahogany."[5] I confess: I'd rather watch movies than read books. I am a writer who doesn't read much beyond the cereal box and my Twitter feed—140 characters or less, excellent portion control. For this reason, don't bother comparing me to some other writer or comedian or feminist or dickhead, or accusing me of plagarism or ignorance. I can tell you right now: I probably don't know what the fuck you're talking about.

Most of these books are Dad's. Books I meant to read but never did because I was too busy seeking the right mousse for curly hair and boys who liked girls with big, orange afros.

I didn't even read half the books on the reading lists of my English classes. They were too big! (Be quiet, husband.) I will name my second child after he who helped me graduate. First name Cole, second name Notes. In my defense, who in the mother has time to read *Vanity Fair* (fattest novel ever) in two days when you're partying five days a week because god is telling you to? Exactly.

---

[5] Oh, Ron Burgundy. You're so very important. (*Anchorman: The Legend of Ron Burgundy*.)

MotherFumbleR

Bye-bye, books. Some will wind up at used bookstores, some will go to teacher friends, and others to coworkers who appreciate a book in the hand while an iPad sits idly by.

John Milton's *Paradise Lost*, an English degree staple. It's time for this classic to get lost.

A Man for All Seasons. No such thing. You're outta here, man.

Shakespeare's *Twelfth Night*. This will be our 7,249th and last night together.

Gone With the Wind. Gone indeed.

The Poetry of John Donne. I am so donne with this one.

I will, however, keep a few books with a particular autograph on the inside cover. I open up a sixty-five-cent copy of *Hamlet* and read, "Jim Combden, 42 Gambier Street." It takes everything in my being to refrain from dialing the phone number Dad printed beneath his address. This is a paperback survivor from the sixties, when he studied English and Shakespeare and poetry and philosophy and cute girls with beehives at Memorial University. This book is a little piece of history from what was surely one of the best times of his life. He penned his name right here on this page I hold in my hand, before marriage and kids and responsibility and cancer were ever in his vocabulary. There is something profound about that. There is the ink. Still bright. Still there. Never fading. A metaphor if I ever heard one.

I will keep this book, and a few others. The husband can turn to page sixty-nine and kiss my ass. Love you, honey. Beer bottles and all.

But the other shit I've collected over the years—it's time to let go. I had a yard sale a while back. It's unbelievable what people will buy from you. One kid bought my *Jeopardy* board game, circa 1989. You know it's old because Alex Trebek's moustache is thick and black. As she carried the game off down the driveway, I yelled, "Remember—Pluto's not a planet anymore, and a Brontosaurus is actually an Apatosaurus now!"

One lady bought a rusty pot for ten cents. I don't even know what to say about that. She was also looking for an electric can opener for her son who just got his own apartment. I asked her,

"Why an electric one?" She said, "Because he is too lazy to turn the handle on the manual one." Wow. Our future is in excellent hands, folks. But don't expect them to actually *use* those hands, except to jerk off all over our hopes and dreams for the future of the universe.

I sold a foot-long pine box that I built in grade nine industrial arts class. On the outside it looked decent—well-made with a little boy and girl carved into the top—but when you opened the lid, BOOM, it hit you in the face: "VICKI 1993," scrawled on the inside of the lid in bright red paint. I joked that I should have put a piece of sandpaper inside the box as a hint that this paint could come off; your name didn't have to be Vicki to enjoy this exquisite vessel of awesomesauce. No need. Just as I was packing away all the unsold crap, a young man pulled up in his car inquiring about kids' stuff. I directed him to a box full of doodads, with my work of art sitting on top of the pile. He grabbed the pine box, said his little girl would love it, and asked me how much I wanted for it. With my aunt- and mother-in-law snickering in the background because I had exclaimed, "He wants my box," I said, "A buck." He threw me a loonie and left with a handful of VICKI 1993. All you need is a handful.

Yard sales are nightmarish. But hey, it was $300 in my pocket that would have gone to the Salvation Army, and don't they have enough musical instruments already? Sheesh.

I admit, I like to hold onto some things. Hard to shake off the teenage girl in me completely. In high school, we kept everything. The REO Speedwagon sticker out of a Hostess potato chip bag because you were eating those chips when you met the first guy who ever touched your boobs. The beer label off a bottle of Red Dog that a really hot guy gave you because everyone knows what that label really means. God teenagers are fucked up. And I was one of them. No worries, all that crap is gone now. Except for maybe most of it. Stay away from that chest with the padlock in my bedroom, Mom! And the numbers written on the back of the padlock are not the right combination, just a decoy, so don't bother trying.

When he calls me a packrat, the thing my husband doesn't

realize is that I have all this shit because I left home when I was eighteen. Not much choice there, people, if you want to do something more than work at the gas station or fish with your uncle. No offense to all ye who work at the gas station or fish with your uncle. I enjoy both gas and fish. Thank you.

So, from age eighteen until the time I bought my house at twenty-three, I was steadily accumulating things. Those five years were prime crap-collecting years for me, unlike my husband who lived with his parents until he met me. When he moved in with his things, he was standing on the front step with a brown paper bag full of socks. (His beer bottle collection would be dropped off later by an eighteen wheeler.)

In my young-adult poverty, I collected things from anyone who'd offer. Sure, I'll take that old toilet seat off your hands. In fact, it's not a toilet seat—it's a table with a hole in the middle. A doughnut table—innovative! Mom and Dad replenished my bank account regularly, but I couldn't use that money for furniture and home décor. That was beer money! And what was left over was money for a new slutty shirt to wear to the Liquordome on Wednesday night. Yes, I said Wednesday.

As you move from piss poor to financial mediocrity you start to shed the junk and replace it with things of quality. But it's a phasing out process. I'm still working on it. Obviously. Here I am in the sweatshirt Dad spilled tea on once as he tried to squeeze around me at the dinner table. It's cute, right? A little bit of dirtbag, a little bit of Lady Macbeth: "Out, damn'd spot! Out, I say!"

Call me a packrat, but this sweater, this stain, and this *Hamlet*, are not going anywhere. Not yet. See, I'm not just playing clutter cop here. I'm sorting though my past, coming face to face with the person I used to be, and deciding what the woman I've become needs to move forward. Like a gambler's hand, it's knowing what to throw away, and knowing what to keep. And I am the only one who can decide that, Kenny Rogers. As much as the mother in me needs to cut the clutter to survive, to that same end there are a few things that, for now, I need to hold onto.

Hold On to Your Dreams.
And Your Dump Truck

Turbo Ginger is a machine. He's go, go, go all day long. Keanu Reeves called last week to see if Max would play his midget protégé in *Speed 3*. I said yes—but only if he'd go back in time and unmake *Sweet November*.

But eventually, even the most sup'd-up motor runs out of steam. When Max finally falls (read: collapses) into a sleeping heap, the tranquility is so resoundingly complete because of the total chaos that came before.

I watch my snow-white sleeping beauty and exhale for the first time in twelve to fourteen hours. I sit on the edge of his bed and take it in. Having gone ten months without more than two hours of unbroken slumber, I will never ever take this sweet stillness for granted. And to that childless crowd who drop by after bedtime and say, "Wake him up, wake him up," I will stab you in the face.

I've kept a journal since I could hold a pen. When I was pregnant, I started writing to Max. Like this entry from October 27, 2008, four months into my pregnancy: "Today we discovered that you are…wait for it, wait for it…a boy!! It's so hard to believe there's a little penis inside me. Again."

I continued to write after he was born, recording all of the details of our new adventures in the Hood. So I decided to revisit those pages, to see what I was writing about during those sleepless nights. The disturbed ramblings of a dog-tired new mother: "My sweet, sweet boy. You had me up all night long, every hour on the hour. I'm so tired, I can't even think straight. But one thing is crystal clear: I love you so much, silly monkey. Yawn." I was clearly delirious, fabricating bliss as a natural defense mechanism to save myself from total and utter madness. I'd like to say it worked, but this being page 198 already, you'd probably beg to differ.

Some kids sleep through the night from week one. Others take months, even years. My friends, Kim and Bruce, have a son who's seven, and every night, without fail, Ryan wakes up, staggers down the hall, and climbs into their bed. He has always done this, so why stop now? They know they've created a monster. In a couple years, they're going to wake up, turn over, and open their sleepy eyes to Ryan's magnificent beard and enormous morning erection. Awkward.

Firemom

"What do you want to be when you grow up, Max?"

He's been asked this question a lot over the last year or so, and his answer has always been the same:

"A fireman," he says, "I want to spout fire."

"Um. Yeah. That would be a *dragon*, honey. Or a pyro. I think maybe you mean you want to *put out* fires."

He nods his head. Phew. I give his fiery mane a tousle, relieved to know he won't be putting the "son" in "arson."

His befuddled job description makes it obvious: this is not a practical decision for Max. He's not choosing to be a fireman because it comes with an excellent benefits package and a sweet pension plan. He wants to be a fireman because he gets to shoot water out of a big hose, drive a shiny red truck with a ladder on top, and save people from burning buildings and, of course, kittens from treetops. Batman is the dark knight. Superman is the man of steel. And Fireman is the great flame slayer! Max doesn't want to "work at a fire station." He wants to be a badass superhero.

He's not alone. Every kid wants to be a hero. They don't skip around the sandbox saying they want to be ad executives or real-estate attorneys or math teachers, as noble as those professions are. They want to be knights and spacemen, princesses and rock stars. Some kids say they want to be doctors and police officers, but that's because they see those jobs as heroic too. They don't want to work (they can barely stand picking up their Legos or brushing their teeth for longer than six seconds). They want adventure and glory. They're not standing up on the coffee table with their hands on their hips and their chests puffed out because they want to be politicians (thank god). "Max, take my red thong off your head right now! That is *not* a helmet."

When I was a little girl, I wanted to be a hero too. Agent Angus MacGyver, specifically. I already had the nape-drape hair. All I needed was a utility knife and some duct tape. And, oh I dunno, maybe an ounce of fine motor skills?

We modify our dreams as we grow to better understand the world. When we're five, we want to grow up and drive the Batmobile. By the time we're fifteen, we know the school bus might be a more viable option. The thing is, dreams are just that—dreams. They seem unrealistic. Farfetched. And some of them are. Unless you have a royal bloodline (or you're swappin' gravies with a prince), you can't be a princess. Unless you live in a comic book, you can't drive Wonder Woman's invisible jet.[6] Unless you're a genius with a vast knowledge of physics, chemistry, lock picking, and defusing bombs with chewing gum, a shoelace, and a paper clip, you can't be MacGyver.

So our dreams shift to more practical pursuits, especially when we become parents. This little person has come along who needs all our attention, all our energy, all our money, and maybe even our will to live. We sacrifice bigger dreams for more reachable ones. Our families come first. Our kids' dreams take precedence over our own.

It's all friggin' fabulous for the first little while, when this little dream come true is all curled up and cooing softly in our arms. But once the novelty of parenthood wears off, when sleep deprivation shakes our sanity and responsibility has us by the short and curlies, we start to feel like failures. Like we haven't accomplished our other dreams, and now—with parenthood kicking us right in the dream-maker and running away laughing like a schoolyard bully—we're never ever gonna. It has swallowed us whole. Any dreams we haven't achieved already are down the toilet, along with the pacifier our kid flushed this morning.

But just because we can't be the warrior ballerina we drew for a

---

[6] For real. Wonder Woman has an invisible jet that leaves her completely visible so she appears to be flying through the air sitting down. I have no idea how she remembers where she parks the thing. But she's Wonder Woman. She figures it out.

poster contest in grade three doesn't mean we can't be heroes. So you wanted to build a robot when you grew up. Well congratulations, sister, you made a living, breathing person with working parts.

We may not be astronomers, but we can lie on a blanket in the backyard and show our kids the constellations. We may not be gladiators, but we can arm wrestle, and lose, at the dinner table. Being a hero doesn't mean you have to be a hero for the world. You can be a hero for one kid's whole world. A real superhero. For one really super kid.

So when you're tempted to use parenthood as your excuse to give up your dreams, remember: some dreams are disguised as ordinary life, with grass stains on their knees and snot on their upper lips.

So I guess I want to be a fireman too (I said *be*, not *do*, pervo). That doesn't mean I want to slide down poles (yes I do) or take frequent catnaps during my shift (yes I do). I mean, metaphorically, I want to be a fireman. Someone Max looks up to, on or off a ladder. The person who runs to his rescue when he ignites the shed with improvised fireworks. I want to stand for something greater in his eyes. I want my actions to speak louder than words, and I want my words to be the truth. Thanks for the lesson, Max, my boy wonder. I want to spout fire too.

As we know by now, the motherhood myth is bullshit. It's supposed to be all butterflies and rainbows, but it's so not. Screw the gag order, the one that says moms can't talk about what pregnancy and labour do to our bodies or what motherhood does to our sense of self. Let's be honest about it. There's excruciating pain, there's stifling stress, there's shit and puke and bruises, there's endless worry. And all this motherfuckery is exactly what makes us heroes. You can't be a hero without a crisis. You can't be a fireman without a fire. Motherhood is about putting out fires as much as it is about cuddling. Sure, Dad's the one with the hose and helmet, but Mom is the one who carries us out of the burning building (that looks a lot like a crotch on fire, because it is a crotch on fire) and brings us into the world.

Moms are heroes. Moms are firemen.

Think about it. You've been to hell and back making this person. You didn't sleep for a bloody year. You're juggling a thousand things at once, putting out fires at every turn, and defusing bombs with nothing more than a wet wipe, a safety pin, and a diaper. You're aware of your own mortality now more than ever, you know pain and survival and compassion, you see the world through the awesome eyes of a child. If these aren't superpowers, I don't know what are. Motherhood is not killing your dreams. It's your flowing red cape and your big sexy S (and ass).

We think motherhood steals away the time we would have spent pursuing greatness, trying to keep up with the men. But maybe it automatically makes us greater. That's not a baby on your back, lady. THAT'S A JET PACK.

Survival:
A Little Crazy Goes a Long Way

So this is it.

The last diaper in the box.

The last drop of milk in the carton.

The last squirt of Canesten in the tube.

The last swig of shiraz in the bottle.

It all runs out at the same damn time, doesn't it? Every couple of months I drop about 400 bucks at the drugstore. And then another fifty at the liquor store. Or is it the other way around? I forget. My head hurts.

Funny how sometimes it all goes to hell at once, and this time I'm not talking about groceries. In a matter of two years, my mom had breast cancer, my dad had colorectal cancer, and I had a baby. My mom lost her right breast and her hair. My dad lost his life. And I lost my mind. Oh, and I got married, so I lost my virginity too.

Hence the lunacy in which these little ditties are steeped. It's called coping. With the wicked pain of childbirth. The paralyzing exhaustion of motherhood. The loss of a father. The ongoing trials of a marriage. The craziness is an essential tool in my Motherhood Survival Kit, right next to my Super Daiquiri Deluxe 3000. So if the eighty-two f-bombs between these covers were a little too much for you, give the author a break. You know—the author. From Vagina, Sasnatchewan. I told you on page one that my coochie wrote this book. But please, cut it some slack. Not that it needs any extra. It's been through a lot. And a lot has been through it.

Motherhood is a Wonderland (Lewis Carroll's, not Michael Jackson's). It's a psychedelic land full of weird little creatures and tweedle-dummies and people screaming, "Off with her head!" You can't hide out in the rabbit hole; you have to get off your arse and fumble your way through the fuckery. You have to find a way to come out on the other end, better than you went in. In this analogy, I suppose you think I'm Alice. But no, darling, Alice I am not: "There is a place. Like no place on Earth. A land full of wonder, mystery, and danger! Some say, to survive it, you need to be as mad as a hatter. Which luckily I am."

By ranting about my battered beaver, I am oddly comforted. Mended, even. Okay not mended, but you get my point. Laughter heals.

By talking about my dead father, he's not dead at all. Writing is the closest thing to a cure for cancer. I keep him alive with the words he taught me to spell.

And don't mistake my rascally ramblings for misery. Just because I'm pissed that I now piss myself every time I cough, it doesn't mean I don't love my son. It's not his fault. It's his father's fault. Off with his head!

My dad is dead and life is hard and marriage sucks ass and the Hood is a scary and uncertain place and we're all going to die, but isn't it fuckin' hilarious? The way I see it, I have two choices: kill myself or laugh hysterically while practicing my kegels to "Kung Fu Fighting." I guess I'll go with number two.

Life is a mother load of pain—for everyone. And truth is, in spite of my broken labia and broken heart, I am a lucky duck. There are parents out there with *real* problems: sick kids, poverty, terrible tragedy, mental illness, and burdensome regret. To them, I surely

sound like an ungrateful wench or like the sociopath mom from *Precious* based on the novel *Push* by Sapphire. I'm sorry. I'm just trying to be funny. If parenthood is not to be laughed at, kill me now.

What's that? You want more chicken soup for the soul? If you insist, here it comes. I'm so thankful for what I have. And I'm thankful for what I've lost, too, because it means I had it once, and I am what I am because of the goodness that lingers. "There is a crack in everything. That's how the light gets in." Leonard fuckin' Cohen.

I am most thankful for what I know. Life is short. Love is everything. Laughter is our lifeblood. And all three of these verbs—live, love, laugh—should never ever be on a poster in your office, a stencil on your wall, or a signature in your email. That's just not cool, man.

I'm mad alright. Mad about a boy with hair like a strawberry sundae, an engine that never stops, and a smile that at once picks me up and makes me fall to pieces.

He is my Yoko Ono. And my Yucky One.

My beautiful doll. And my Savage Patch Kid.

My muse. And my mutant from the planet Poopiter.

Stealer of my heart. Breaker of my heart-shaped box.

My raison d'etre and the reason we're out of raisins.

My whole life. And my early grave.

He is the reason I don't completely hate the world, because he is in it.

And the reason I get up every morning, psychotic but psyched, to fumble through the darkness.

BIB-LABIA-GRAPHY

The line "Life's a journey, not a destination," quoted on page 51, is taken from the Aerosmith song "Amazing" which appears on their 1993 album *Get a Grip*. The line has also been attributed to the American poet and philosopher Ralph Waldo Emerson. Page 77 quotes David Bowie's "Changes" from the album *Hunky Dory* (1971). The stanza from Christopher Morley's poem "To a Child," on page 89, comes from his collection *Chimneysmoke* (1921). On page 120, the quoted line comes from the 1987 film *Dirty Dancing*. The quoted lines on page 123 are from The Bee Gees song "Tragedy" from the album *Spirits Having Flown* (1979). The mis-transcribed lines on page 165 are based on song lyrics from "Livin' on a Prayer" and "You Give Love a Bad Name" by Bon Jovi from the album *Slippery When Wet* (1986). The quote from Ron Burgundy on page 170 is from the 2004 film *Anchorman: The Legend of Ron Burgundy*. The quoted lines on page 186 are from Phil Collins's song "Against All Odds (Take a Look at Me Now)" from the *Against All Odds* soundtrack (1984). The lines from William Blake on page 192 are from his poem "Auguries of Innocence" from *The Pickering Manuscript* (c. 1807). And the quoted lines on page 203 are from Lewis Carroll's *Alice's Adventures in Wonderland* (1865).

ACKNOWLEDGMENTS

Earlier versions of some of the stories in this book appeared on my blog *motherblogger.ca*, on the *Huffington Post*, and in *Today's Parent* magazine.

THANKS...

To Mom, for taking care of everything so I could finish this book at her kitchen table. To Dad, for giving me the courage. To ever-patient Andrew, for letting me do my thang. To Kim, for telling me to write more than long-winded emails. To Gary, for making me "walk through the art room naked." To Kristian, for telling me to "just be Vic." To Darrin, Irene, Robin, Michael and all my advisors at m5, for your delicious brains. And to everyone who gave me blog and tech support, whose names could fill up a second book. To David, for the saucy ginger snaps. To Rebecca, Elisabeth, Rhonda, and the staff at Breakwater, for breaking my water. To James, for helping me give birth to this screaming, brazen thing. To Chad, for showing me I could do it too. To the Combdens, Staggs, and Murphys, for laughing at me and with me. To everyone who reads my stuff and shares the love, for reminding me that we are not alone. To women who refuse to be quiet. To moms who rule the world. And to my amazing Max, for being the cause, the cure, the heart, the soul, the everything. I love you like crazy.

All photos of Vicki Murphy by David Howells.

VICKI MURPHY is a self-described "writer, mother, and hot mess" from Badger's Quay, Newfoundland. She is an advertising creative director, a frequent *Huffington Post* contributor, and the creator of the popular blog *motherblogger.ca* – where Vicki chronicles her misadventures in motherhood. She lives in St. John's, Newfoundland, with her husband, Andrew, and their son, Max.